With All My Soul

A pilgrimage to love

Pamela O'Cuneen

Chiselbury

Published by Chiselbury Publishing, a division of Woodstock Leasor Limited, 14 Devonia Road, London N1 8JH, United Kingdom

www.chiselbury.com

The moral right of Pamela O'Cuneen to be identified as the author of this work is asserted.

ISBN: 978-1-916556-67-6 (hardback)

ISBN: 978-1-908291-68-3 (epub)

Cover design by Jane Hannath

Dedicated to Kieran, my soulmate.

CONTENTS

PROLOGUE

This book has taken many years of thought and procrastination. How to write such a story? Where to begin? Should it be in the first person? Should it be fictionalised to protect the writer and the characters? Finally, a traumatic event became a catalyst, and caused pen to be put to paper, in the knowledge that there are more important issues than privacy or stylistic quibbles and in the knowledge too that my beloved very much wanted the story to be told.

It is a story about love.

There are many kinds of love. We all experience more than one kind in the course of a lifetime. Perhaps reading this book will give an inkling of what might be, and will inspire some to stay open to the possibility of a deep and lifelong love, one which transforms lives, outlasts separation and is deeper and more real at the end than at the beginning.

And perhaps also to the possibility that love is eternal and might be, in the end, all that matters and the underpinning of everything that is.

Thanks to all those who have supported and encouraged this story, and to our many friends and guides along the way, some of whom appear in the narrative. My helpful and encouraging readers, Gry Iverslein Katz, Mary Clews, Roisin O'Connor- Laurence, and Lesley Perry all made positive suggestions. Gratitude to Richard Addis who has been an encouraging presence since the beginning of my writing career, and to Laura Palmer, who fell in love with the book and became both publishing mentor and friend. And in the latter stages, a bow to the brilliant graphic designer Jane Hannath, virtuoso of the computer and to my publisher Stuart Leasor, whose relaxed warmth has made the production of the book such a pleasant process. May its message go out into the world.

THE APPLE TREE POEM

Break the fruit from the apple tree, love,
Take, bite and eat,
Fresh the juice in our kisses, love,
Cool grasses splash our feet.

A bleak space bare of apples, love,
Black spikes hung with crows,
Beneath the snow and ashes, love,
There's life that stirs and grows.

An orchard pink with blossom, love,
Ten thousand seas of greeting,
And a golden apple summer, love,
Seed sacrifice completing.

Pamela O'Cuneen Perugia, 1968

1
THE MAGIC OF BOOKS

When I was five I baptised the cat. Rufus was a large tabby with black stripes. He was deeply displeased but I explained that I was anxious for his immortal soul as I poured water over him and said the magic words which I had found in a book. He was not at all grateful.

I had begun school at the local convent. Fascinated by this small school since kindergarten days, I would stop to look through the wire fence at the children in their brown pleated uniforms. It was a pleasant surprise when Mother announced that I would go there at the age of 5 to learn to be a lady, as she had done in a small country convent in the hot, dry North West of Western Australia. I discovered early on that in the convent school I was something called a "non catholic" which seemed to be a category of non-being rather than of being. It never occurred to me that this was a disadvantage or that I would end up anywhere other than heaven – with Rufus the cat of course. There was a lot to learn, reading, writing, manners, music, sewing, drawing and religion. I scampered home after the first day, and proudly demonstrated the sign of the cross, and the "Hail Mary" as we had been taught. This was not well received. It was not what Mother had intended since she had instructed me to "Take all the religion with a grain of salt". Why salt? That was the problem with grownups. They so often said things that made no sense at all.

The nuns were kindly women. They wore black floor length habits and veils with a white collar, like neat black cats with touches of white. As we never saw their legs we assumed they didn't have any, and as we never saw them eat we imagined they didn't need to do that either, though they did sometimes emerge from their private room after break, smelling mysteriously of tea and biscuits. Classes were well taught, without a great deal of imagination, but as we didn't know anything at all, it was all new to us and usually interesting, if puzzling at times. If we fell over on the hard asphalt playground tears would be dried, wounds would be washed, and we would sit on a warm black-clad knee to have the wound painted with purple disinfectant before running off to play again. Somehow we never made the connection that perhaps they had legs after all. Bad behaviour was sometimes called "A Pauling", but no-one ever explained who Paul was. It was a school regime that marched in lines but within the pattern there was fun to be had.

Growing up in Western Australia, the days were a joyous succession of sunlit discoveries. Most of the discoveries reinforced my conviction that the world was a glorious place. Red grapes hanging from the long trellis on the way to the outside dunny, figs and lemons and loquats there in the garden for the picking, kookaburras that cackled their raucous song and magpies fluting and bubbling in the garden every morning. But sometimes the paradisal idyll was ruptured – a bobtail goanna might unexpectedly open his mouth and hiss with a blue tongue, or the sweet figs from the fig tree would need to be examined very carefully in case there was a wriggling worm inside. The suburban garden of one third of an acre was a whole universe. It contained every world that a child's imagination could conjure up. A visit to the circus turned the swing into a trapeze, and Rufus became a tiger. A visit to the theatre produced plays for a line-up of dolls. Audrey, pink rabbit, Marie Louise and Lucy were an attentive audience. They could be sung to, taught and chastised.

Summers were an astonishment of heat. When the temperature climbed the house was closed and blinds were drawn. But a child could lie outside on the coarse dark green lawn, underneath the shade of a jacaranda tree, looking up at the blue, blue sky through the leaves and branches and drifting off into a dream. When the hot evenings came, people came out into their gardens with hoses to cool off the parched plants. Sometimes Rufus the cat would be accidentally watered and would come out from under a bush, wet, spiky and incensed. Mother, Dad and I would stand by the green side gate, waiting for the sea breeze, called the Fremantle Doctor, to arrive from the West, feeling the first breath cooling our sweaty faces as it ruffled our hair. On hot, hot nights we might take a rug out into the garden to lie on our backs, watching the moon and chatting, mindful of Mother's warning that "If you go to sleep with the moon on your face you will have seven years bad luck!" The same, it seemed would happen if we broke a mirror or spilled the salt, and to this day I surreptitiously throw a pinch over my left shoulder if the latter happens.

Mother was a slim pretty woman who seemed to me to be the essence of all that womanhood should be. She was a lady. She wore high heels, and a a hat and gloves when she went to church or to town. She was endlessly busy in the house where every object had its allotted place and dared not move an inch. Dusting was done every day and floor polishing once a week. When the first roaring vacuum cleaner arrived both Rufus and I fled in terror. Before Dad came home from his office in town in the evening Mother would put on lipstick and a pretty dress, and we would wait to hear the sound of his smartly marching feet down the road, and the unique musical squeak of the front gate. I welcomed Dad not only for the pleasure of having his cheerful presence at home but for what he might bring in his brown case. It might be new books from the library in town, or a piece of cheese, or on a Saturday, a bag of sweets to be eaten while we listened to the radio.

Radio was the entertainment for families in those days. We would gather round to listen to the news. We were children of the Commonwealth and Empire, and this was an Australia where some still referred to Britain as 'Home'. We always listened first to the important Overseas News announced by Big Ben, followed by the local news. Dad loved the comedy shows like "Much Binding in the Marsh" though we never dreamed that there could really be quaint places in England with names like that.

There were quiz shows subsidised by soap companies where the prize would be an 'overseas trip'. As the compere read out the magical places the prizewinner would visit the names resonated in my child's mind, evoking enchanted images. It seemed that by answering more questions the contestant could travel further and further. It wasn't clear what would happen if they only went as far as Singapore or Ceylon – would they be stranded there forever? But to us, the magical destination where all things were golden, was London. The dreamlike mirage of "Overseas Travel" shimmered in an unattainable future. It was almost "The undiscovered country from whose bourne no traveller returns," as Hamlet would have it, and the few that did return, merited an awed and hushed audience for their slide shows.

School, like life, was an endless parade of interesting things to be learned. Reading was a world that suddenly opened up a magical door. One day letters were mysterious shapes, with b and d sworn enemies, and then suddenly the patterns fell into place, and everything, from jam jars to newspaper headlines made the world an endless puzzle to be solved. Very soon it was impossible to find enough to read, and I devoured every book in the adult bookshelves, discovering that sometimes even the most boring and dusty volume could contain an exciting story, and that long words could be skipped over or guessed at in the interests of the next exciting event.

There were few childrens' books post war and those were handed down from cousins or aunts. Someone produced a floppy book called "Popsy's Party" which struck me, at 4 or 5 as extremely childish, as were the ballet classes where a Joyce Grenfell lookalike exhorted us to "Be little bunny rabbits".

Those were the days when childhood diseases were something to be caught and done with. A bout of measles brought deliverance from the need to be a bunny rabbit in the Christmas concert, and introduced me to the joys of the "Wind in the Willows" read aloud. It was an unillustrated volume. There was no way an Australian child could know what a mole, a badger, a stoat or a weasel might look like, and yet by the power of words alone, I entered entranced into that green and misty world created by Kenneth Grahame, and have loved it for a lifetime. I admired the swashbuckling and confident Ratty, but secretly empathised a lot more with dear little introverted and emotional Mole. To this day, when a picnic is unpacked I see him raising his paws and saying, "Oh my!" and hear him enumerating the the wonders of the picnic spread. And I cannot see a picture of a toad or a vintage car without saying "poop poop" under my breath. But the passage and the scene that took me beyond myself was always "The Piper at the Gates of Dawn" when Ratty and Mole hear mysterious music and find the lost baby Otter lying at the feet of Pan.

"Then suddenly Mole felt a great Awe fall upon him, an awe that turned his muscles to water, bowed his head, and rooted his feet to the ground. It was no panic terror – indeed he felt wonderfully at peace and happy – but it was an awe that smote and held him and, without seeing, he knew it could only mean that some august Presence was very, very near….." It was an early introduction to a world beyond everyday life, a world where mysticism and magic might be real. I never forgot that passage. Who can know how stories and phrases read to us as children can set the course of a lifetime's searching?

At the end of seven years it was time to go to secondary school. This involved a change of uniform to a sky-blue tunic, a blazer and a straw hat. The new school was also run by the same Loreto nuns. They were mostly motherly and kind. There were some we considered cross or 'crabby'. Only in retrospect is one able to see these women more clearly, as once pretty girls with dreams and boyfriends, who had given up their lives to take vows of poverty, chastity and obedience, and who may have been more or less happy with the resulting life options. Some seemed extremely happy. But like all children, we judged our teachers and the other adults in our lives purely by how their behaviour impinged on our own desires and freedom with no ability to extend our empathy beyond our own feelings. It is one measure of maturity when that becomes possible.

And the unfailing way of extending one's empathy, was through reading voraciously, through every class library, through the bookshelves at home, at the grandparents' house, books on the shelves of uncles and aunts. Christmas was not Christmas without one or two new books. The great joy after Christmas lunch was to lie on the bed in the afternoon heat, lost in the new stories. My best friend at school proved to be a black-haired and bespectacled girl called Christine who greeted me, on the first day with

"Have you got any books at home? I'm coming to see you".

Christine indeed loved books as much as I did, and even better, had a subscription to her local library. We would be friends for life.

Reading opened new and unknown worlds. While reading stories we absorb other countries, cultures and landscapes. We travel in the mind to hot and cold countries and experience worlds of emotion that we had never dreamt of. We learn how other people live and think, and learn, by comparison what we think. And in some ways, sadly we learn what the world thinks we ought to think. We learn what is admired in the fields of art, literature and music, and if we are new and unsure in those worlds, we try to model our taste on what seems to be admired. Sometimes we are moved and inspired by what we find, sometimes we are not and feel guilty and inadequate for what must surely be our lack of appreciation, but mostly we dive into the riches that the printed word has to offer and our imaginations are stimulated and awakened. Reading teaches us not only what other people and other places are like, but where we stand in relation to them, and we somehow piece together the person that we will become from the kaleidoscope of images that begins to populate our mind.

I began to dream of life overseas. From Primary school onwards, even elementary reading books were imported from England. They had illustrations of bare trees and cottages like a child's drawings, and seasons that were the reverse of those we experienced. As an avid reader I came to the conclusion that since whatever was in books must be correct, there was something inferior and wrong with Australia, and that the sooner I could go to the other side of the world where daffodils bloomed at Easter, blackbirds and thrushes sang and Christmas was snowy and cold, the better. It was a commonly held view that Australia somehow didn't count. Later termed the 'Australian cringe', our colonial mindset discounted much of the beauty and real talent around us, and modelled ourselves largely on northern hemisphere values. Yes, we had our bush poets, and a few novelists, but writers, musicians, artists and actors were only truly valued if they had been 'overseas' and found success there. Then they were worshipped and feted on their triumphant return.

Literature and music became the passions of my life. From the age of 11, when "One Fine Day" from Puccini's "Madame Butterfly" was sung on the radio before school as Mother brushed my long hair, I was bitten with the opera bug. Sunday afternoons were spent twiddling the radio knobs to find programmes of opera favourites which I listened to avidly with Kobbe's "Complete Opera Book" open on my lap for the stories, although the monochrome pictures of large busted Brunnhildes did little to convey the colour of a stage performance. Slowly I began to realise that by some magic of the vocal cords I too could produce a sound like that and spent many happy hours imitating prima donnas. Piano practice became another passion, and like many musical adolescents I imagined myself on the concert platform, and practised for hours – although the tedium of scales was helped by propping a story book on the music stand until Mother smelled a rat.

School days were happy, as they tend to be for those of us fortunate enough to be amenable to following rules and able to pass regular tests. And tests and exams there were, three times a year, all studied for and executed as though a place at Oxford or Cambridge depended on them. Although religion did not figure large at home in our mildly Anglican family, I was particularly interested in Religious Education and always scored high marks, which resulted in mild scoldings for the rest of the class, that this outsider should outshine them. Religious instruction consisted in much learning of catechism questions. It produced well educated parrots who had not necessarily thought about or analysed the subject matter at depth. Nevertheless, we imbibed moral values and above all a spirit of kindness and generosity.

Times of prayer and silence in chapel were meaningful. When I was 11, an elderly uncle suffered a heart attack. There was an atmosphere of dread and chaos in the family. I knew from the nuns at school that prayer was required, so while the family sat in frightened silence in the hospital waiting room I quietly set myself to pray for Uncle Jack. As the days went by I visited the Holy Rosary Church up the road and sat in the empty dark-wood pews, listening to the cool silence and almost imagining that the blue robes of the virgin's plaster statue were moving gently in the breeze. Dropping deeper into the silence I realised that this deep spirituality felt like home – and because the most meaningful spirituality I had met so far was Catholicism, a longing to become a catholic took deep root in my being. Later, with exposure to other cultures and world religions there would be other avenues to explore, but not so in the 1960s. From the age of 11, through teenage years, this desire persisted. With a mother who had the "take religion with a grain of salt" mentality, such an idea would have been anathema and it remained unspoken.

Overcoming real terror at endangering the status quo, I arranged afternoon tea at the convent in the summer holidays, and in the silent, hot 'visitor's parlour' smelling of beeswax, talked about my desire with a favourite nun, Mother Benignus, who had a stern face with a straight mouth, but a soft heart. With a quiet smile, she advised me to wait. So wait I did, through seemingly endless years, reading and wishing for the time when I could be free to make my own decisions.

Perhaps the position of outsider meant that I felt it was necessary to try harder with God. Did I feel that I would never make the heavenly grade however much I longed to? I am not sure. I only know that I sensed something very real behind the nuns' spirituality, something that was not much in evidence in the world outside. Kindness, good deeds and the possibility of 'sin' were part of common parlance, though I never felt particularly sinful. But in general, during the years of waiting we just carried on with learning and homework, tennis and chatting like any normal schoolgirls – although perhaps we convent girls were a bit more conscious of being well behaved, and of the necessity of wearing regulation hats and gloves when in school uniform.

The science of good behaviour extended, in senior years, to sex, which was only obliquely mentioned, and 'going out with boys' was presented as being fraught with unknown perils. Since these things were only hinted at the lectures were more confusing than enlightening. Perhaps those with brothers who were closer in age than mine had more realistic knowledge, but to the rest of us, protected as we were, boys were an unknown and slightly unsavoury quantity which made the 'end of school dance' an ordeal to be feared. Having negotiated the hurdles of the first lipstick and high heels, we had to run the gauntlet of being asked to dance and the awful trial of being piloted around a dance floor by a real live boy. No longer just the rainy day fun of learning the Barn dance, the waltz and the Maxina in the school hall while dear old Mother Gertrude pounded out the tunes with fingers worn spatulate by years of piano-playing. And worse, we would have to talk to them. One technique was to memorise five or six questions to begin a conversation. This seemed to work until I was asked to dance a second time by the same boy. It proved impossible to remember which questions I had already used! The conversation ground to a halt and we concentrated ferociously on our feet.

With matriculation done, and final music exams passed there was just one more long hot summer holiday before University began. It had never occurred to me that I would not go to University. My much older brother, my prince and my mother's pride and joy, had studied science there and it seemed the logical next step. There was a bewildering array of subjects to choose from, many of them setting off exciting sequences of thought as I imagined what it would be like to study this or that discipline and where it might lead.

The University of Western Australia was based on the Scottish system whereby students studied a reducing number of subjects at increasing depth over three years for the basic bachelors degree. Though passionate about music, I opted for English, French, Philosophy and Economics.

Looking at first year university students today I realise how young we were – in Australia the age for beginning 'Uni' was 17. Some of us were barely that. Agog for new learning and experience, socially inept and shy outside the convent shelter, life became an exercise in appearing far more confident that I was. In those days, the University of Western Australia had just 2,000 students, housed on a flowering campus with sun-soaked Tuscan style central buildings, and a motley selection of temporary structures stretching across the fields. We did as much walking as studying and slowly took the measure of our lecturers, who were mostly from Britain, and of other students, who were as raw as ourselves. What none of us knows at that age is that 99 out of 100 of one's fellow students are also feeling out of their depth and probably struggling just as hard.

Everything was new- the experience of having lectures dotted throughout the week, being handed reading lists to organise for ourselves, and the first experience of 'tutorials'. What were they? And what were we meant to discuss when we didn't yet have informed opinions about anything?

Some lecturers were frightening, some reassuring, some white-haired and some not much older than we were. The first-year philosophy lecturer was a tall bespectacled young man who seemed permanently attached to a microphone with a long cord. He walked up and down, kicking the cord around as though it was a train behind him. When students complained of the distraction he obliged by sitting in the lotus pose on his lectern for the next lecture. One English Literature lecturer, a tubby little man from northern England, delighted in shocking first year students with the more ribald poems of Pope and Dryden, and shocked us even more by criticising Dickens, whom we had thought to be next only to the Bible and Shakespeare in the hierarchy of excellence. Our French teacher wore white Heidi plaits around her head and was obsessed with French phonetics – for which I later had cause to thank her. She was a pioneer of language laboratories when such things were unheard of. The Economics lecturer, a brilliant man, was blind and came to lectures with his black Labrador guide dog- a wonderful distraction for inattentive students.

There were, of course myriad distractions. Some students became caught up in romances, some spent their time in the Dramatic Society, or the Rowing Club, others became library hermits. I did little other than study, and made tentative relationships with a few more conservative peers. And outside University, I began singing lessons with Lucie Howell, red haired and stern, the doyenne of singing teachers in our small city. It meant weekly lessons in a small studio, and strict daily practice in a way that took much of the joy out of singing. But there were also choirs at the University and the opportunity to sing beautiful music under the baton of excellent musicians. The works we learned, the madrigals, the motets, the Indian Queen by Purcell, Bach's St Matthew Passion, were all absorbing and became lifelong and much loved inhabitants of an inner musical treasure-house.

In the second year of University I fell in love. It was not with a fellow student but with Gerard Manley Hopkins, the 19th century Jesuit poet who changed the course of English poetry and, while puzzling his contemporaries greatly, opened later poets' eyes to the intricacies of 'sprung rhythm', the essential 'selfhood' of nature, and the passion and struggles of the dark night of the soul. Just the sort of thing to appeal to an unconfident, sensitive convent-educated student. Carrying the slim volume of his verse around, I would walk through the university gardens, saying his poetry to myself, eulogising skylarks, and windhovers, poplars and mountain streams:

"When weeds, in wheels, shoot long and lovely and lush
Thrush's eggs look little low heavens, and thrush
Through the echoing timber does so rinse and wring
The ear, it strikes like lightnings to hear him sing."

None of this had we ever seen or experienced. It was a kind of drunkenness on sensibility and religious experience, and the continuation of a lifelong love affair with everything in the Northern Hemisphere.

Also during that second year I discovered the oneness of knowledge. Studying English literature, with its heavy reliance on classical themes, Greek and French Drama, Corneille and Racine (Oh Andromache, Oh Phedre!) suddenly all these different worlds coalesced and in a lightning flash a tapestry of relationships and interweaving influences appeared. It was a revelation, since up to that point lessons had been tied up in neat little parcels labelled English, History, Geography, Music – now suddenly they all began interacting in a miraculous dance.

This was intensified in the third year, when a landscape of endless reading opened out. The syllabus seemed to entail everything that had ever been written, from Daniel Defoe to James Joyce, from Christopher Marlowe to Arthur Miller, and from Chaucer to T.S. Eliot. And it was with the latter that I had my third-year love affair.

The expansiveness of Eliot's vision opened up vistas of world culture that I had never dreamed of, and certainly could not begin to understand from a modest suburban Australian background. Copies of the poems were covered with endless pencilled notes, as our erudite and very British tutor toiled through Eliot's literary and historical references. Suddenly lecturers seemed to be speaking a foreign language as they abandoned simplification for challenge in their approach to us and credited us with a comprehension we did not have. The glimpses of a world view far beyond Perth, Western Australia, were both mystifying and enticing. Just as every section of the University library seemed to open up into a dream-like maze of tunnels, so every quote in Eliot's poetry hinted at some realms of which we had no knowledge. And above all, the Four Quartets appealed, those misty and mystical evocations of eternity, seen through the lens of the longed-for, rain-washed land of England. I was drawn to the concept of life as a journey and an exploration, with no end other than to lead back to a conscious knowledge of our own beginnings.

Parallel to these studies was a continuing interest in things of the spirit. During University years my good friend Christine, she of the books, underwent a violent conversion from Catholicism to extreme evangelical Christianity. From a teenage black stockinged beatnik, she metamorphosed overnight into a strait-laced evangelist, face devoid of makeup, hair dragged back, flat shoes on her feet, and a terrifying lethal bible under one arm which she aimed with martial accuracy at anyone unwise enough to engage in conversation with her. As fearful for her immortal soul as I had been for Rufus' I set myself to reconvert her to Catholicism. She had the same fears for me, and out of love and friendship we engaged in spiritual duelling over the course of a year or so, trading theological repartee with deadly undergraduate seriousness.

She prevailed upon me to attend her church, a red brick building on a highway, where the congregation indulged in an interminable hymn sandwich, and where, every time a text was announced, there was an eager rustling of bibles in a kind of race to display the utmost devotion and familiarity with Holy Writ.

Then came a night when I stayed with her at her sister's house near the ocean. We were warned not to go out late into the streets in case there were some Saturday night revellers. There was no chance of that. Christine embarked on her mission to 'convert' me, and set about it with gusto and bucketfuls of Biblical texts. We fenced and parried theology and pseudo theology for hours until finally in the early hours of the morning I found myself saying an exhausted "Yes" to I hardly knew what.

The next morning dawned sunny and bright blue as only a morning in Western Australia can be, and I awoke to a transformed world. It was as though the lens of a camera had shifted from monochrome to technicolour and soft focus as well. Every shaft of light was exquisite, every leaf, every flower, every note of birdsong or music was transformed into something paradisiacal. It was as though I had never lived before and scales had dropped from my eyes. I understood the meaning of the experience Thomas Traherne described in "Centuries of Meditations":

"The dust and stones of the street were as precious as gold: the gates were at first the end of the world. The green trees when I saw them first through one of the gates transported and ravished me, their sweetness and unusual beauty made my heart to leap, and almost mad with ecstasy, they were such strange and wonderful things:…"

It was as Traherne described it, the light over everything was radiant, both soft and golden, music sounded heavenly with overtones I had never heard before, everything seemed to have a kind of aureole around it. This state of bliss lasted for three days, fading slowly, until life and vision returned to normal.

It was inexplicable but unforgettable, as though the word "Yes" had opened a door into another dimension, one which was always there though not always accessible.

I would discover some years later that saying "Yes," could bring about not only exquisite beauty but exquisite and agonising suffering and that it was necessary to say "Yes" to both. Once embarked on a path of spiritual searching there is no way of predicting the direction that path will take, the discoveries along the way or the sacrifices it will involve. And it seems that one is held on a long leash, twitched if we stray too far away from that path.

Some time later, near the end of the degree course, I found myself musing that I had never experienced what it was like not to have faith in Western Christianity, or a belief in the Divine. In a moment of extraordinary daring or perhaps insanity I prayed to understand what it might be to be outside that magic circle of security. And in the next days and weeks it was as though from being secure inside a safe cathedral with bright stained glass windows, I found myself an outcast, looking at the building from the outside, where the stone was hard and grey and the stained glass was colourless and meaningless. The childhood God of comfort and kindness was transformed almost overnight into a Deity of power and distance, a source of energy but no light, a mysterious force with whom it was possible to make any relationship at all.

The suffering was intense. While studying for finals in English Literature I found my deepest self in an abyss of doubt and incomprehension, unable to grasp any thread linking back to the certainties that had gone before.

Writing for help to the same beloved and trusted nun I had consulted aged 11, I was directed to Father Ted Stormon, a gentle balding Jesuit scholar of languages and medieval literature. He was the rector of the Thomas More men's residential college at the University. I attended his lectures on provencal literature. He would speak with eyes to the ceiling, as though he was seeing visions, or perhaps he was just very shy. With terror, I approached him and embarked on a series of discussions sitting on the couch in his study. Poor Ted Stormon, my bewilderment must have been as bewildering to him as it was to me, as I struggled to understand again what God was, and what faith and spirituality might be from my new position outside the pale. Years passed, and the searching and reading continued, while with monumental patience my mentor continued to answer unanswerable questions.

In the meantime, graduation happened, and a Diploma in Education was obtained, and I went out into the world as a teacher in secondary schools. The system in the West Australian Education department required teachers who had been financially supported during their studies to teach for an equivalent number of years in any country area to which they might be sent. In my case the destination was an inland wheat belt town called Merredin, 160 miles from Perth. No accommodation was provided. Scouring the town, room and board were found with a kindly bustling woman who lived in a small wooden house with a corrugated iron roof. The rooms heated up so violently in the high wheat belt temperatures that I would put my nightclothes in the fridge before bed. During the summer days the flat red earth scorched. The school was built in square quadrangles down which the wind whistled in the winter. And teaching was not what I had imagined it to be – enlightening young minds. At the very mention of the word "poetry" teenage boys made vomiting noises from the back of the class. I discovered that

High School education was largely about keeping order and lived in fear of being unable to quell an incipient riot. As my nickname in the school was "Powder puff" it was evident that I was not regarded as any kind of strict disciplinarian. The days became a torment as I struggled to do a job for which I was almost completely unsuited. Standing in front of a class felt like being eaten alive by ants. At the worst times, on the long trips to and from the city, I would pray to be hit by an oncoming car so that it could all end and there would be no class to face on Monday morning. And yet over the year, some kind of accommodation was reached. I eventually found that rather than shouting at the classes as some teachers did, I could charm them with laughter, and we began to declare a truce.

My passion for music and singing had little outlet, and singing lessons were 160 miles away in Perth. This meant trips in the tiny green mini minor every second weekend just for the nourishment of a singing lesson, and long hours practising in an isolated wing of the school at night, with a badly tuned piano, while the metal stays on the school flag-pole clanged and clattered dementedly in the wind.

The year in Merredin passed, the summer holidays came and the teacher's transfer list was published. I found myself transferred to another country town, Moora, only 103 miles from Perth. It seemed close by comparison. Here I boarded on a farm with a tall laconic farmer and his congenial and cultured wife. They had two daughters at boarding school and a delightful 9 year old son. With Courtney, the farmer's wife I shared books and painted sunsets, while little Hamish and I had adventures together in the creek, rescued magpies, fed orphan lambs and chased errant sheep. The area had a large aboriginal population and as a city dweller I began to learn something about the contrasting world views of white Europeans and indigenous Australians. Despite earnest and unremitting effort by a team of specially allocated teachers to design a programme for these students, by the end of the year it became apparent that very little that was being taught was relevant or meaningful to these young people as they became progressively more bored and disenchanted with what the European education system had to offer.

Then, with mixed joy and regret, I was transferred back to the capital city, Perth, to a High School in a newly built and expensive area by the ocean. The proximity of the school to the ocean meant that unruly and daring boys tended to come back to class after lunch with wet hair, having secreted their surf boards in the sand dunes. I realised then that the problems and behaviour of over privileged young people did not differ much from those who were denied their advantages.

One day, during that year, drying up as Mother washed the dishes, I was idly chasing rainbows in the detergent foam when an idea came to me. Scores of young Australians, including many of my friends were going to that magical land "Europe" on "two year working holidays". I was suddenly struck by the thought- "I could do that too!" and like St Paul being struck from his horse, the light dawned and the world changed.

A plan was formed to go to Europe as soon as the three years of teaching bond ended. The years of teaching in tiny country towns had netted sufficient savings for an airfare to Europe and enough money to live frugally for a year. I was introduced to Madame Ladomirska, a language teacher from one of the local girls' colleges, who was planning a "Grand Tour" with half a dozen girls, in a cultural gap year, and was happy for me to join as a kind of sub-chaperone. The group would leave Australia in January, and I would join them in April after resigning from teaching. We would spend three months in Paris, enrolled in the "Cours de Civilisation" at the Sorbonne, and three months studying

Italian at the Università per Stranieri in Perugia. Given my interest in languages and passion for Italian opera and singing it seemed ideal.

I began learning Italian from a grammar book during the hot summer holidays and took pronunciation lessons from an ancient German language teacher whose cluttered dark room smelled of pipe smoke and tobacco. This was not enough so having enrolled in Italian at the university every afternoon after school was spent rushing to the university for Mass and a fond hello to Ted Stormon, and an hour in the French language laboratory followed by one or two hours of congenial Italian lectures. The tyres of my beloved green Mini Minor ran hot with energy.

I approached Father Ted Stormon to ask if now, before I left for Europe, he would consider receiving me into the Church. He took a week to consider it, prayerfully I imagine. When the answer came it was as much a surprise to me as it would have been to those who imagined the Catholic Church as a ravening maw ingesting converts.

The answer was "No".

"You must learn to trust", he said. "You have to go on this journey like a pilgrimage and find your way."

I went home, shocked and disappointed. The only thing I could think of doing was to kneel by the side of my bed, bury my face in the mattress and pray over and over again "Thy Will be Done." After what seemed a very long time I surfaced and got up, surprised to feel complete calm and acceptance, and joined my parents for the evening meal.

Preparations for the trip continued. Exciting airline bookings were made and luggage bought. Friends came with presents they thought for some reason might be useful – folding slippers, a heavy hardback copy of the newly published "Dutch Catechism", and horror of horrors, a large and cumbersome "Travelling Wardrobe" from my elderly aunt who thought it would be just what was needed. This contraption, in which she kept her beady-eyed fox fur, was a diabolically heavy plastic container for coats, with space for several coat-hangers. It was like travelling with a man-size body bag, and haunted my every move for months to come.

When the time came to break the news, with atypical chutzpah, I gathered my courage, made an appointment to see the High School Headmaster, waltzed in and said, "Mr Wilson, isn't it wonderful? I'm going to Paris on 8th April!"

The poor man was so surprised he could only agree.

2
THE WINGS OF THE MORNING

Turning my back on Perth's squat airport building with its small ornamental pool of black swans, I boarded the Air India plane. Mind full of memories of childhood, pounding heart full of expectation of adventure and the unknown, I was on the way to the Europe of my imagination. It was April 1968, and I was 26. It was the culmination of years of reading and longing.

The plane took off. Parents on the viewing platform decreased in size with frightening speed as I left childhood behind. As I looked down, I thought in a moment of panic – "What have I done? Should we be this high above the ground?" I was flying alone in a plane full of strangers. Everything I had ever known was receding. Nothing familiar was ahead – only the imagined and as yet unknown.

Opening my capacious 1960s handbag, I took out a little soft-covered burgundy book, "Prayers from the Psalms". It had been a present from my favourite nun, mentor and friend. It fell open at Psalm 139:

"Though I take the wings of the morning and fly to the uttermost parts of the sea,
Still Thou art with me and Thy right hand upholds me."

It was comforting. It seemed like an omen. I hoped it was. Later in my travels I would come upon the Rodin sculpture of the hand of God – two lovers curled together in the palm of a huge hand. It too would become a treasured symbol of trust and security.

But for now, I was nervous, excited, and ready to meet the world in a state of naive and raw expectation. The hostesses were wearing silk saris in jewel colours. The menu offered Indian or Western food. Suddenly western food seemed beige and bland. The walls were decorated with orange lotus flowers and convoluted camels waving their necks in a dance. For the first time I experienced what would become a lifelong precious sensation, that of being in mid-air, anonymous and free.

The flight landed in Singapore, during a tropical rain shower. Small men with brightly painted Chinese umbrellas escorted passengers from the plane. In the Cathay Hotel a pianist played "Lara's Theme" on a white grand piano surrounded by banks of flowers. The south-east asian food, a simple bowl of noodles with aromatic ginger, chilli and lime, was like nothing I had ever experienced before. It tasted like heavenly nectar and the bed was soft and enormous.

The following day I boarded an Air France flight to Paris. It was an old Caravelle plane, and travelling in economy class, the emphasis was on economy rather than "class" Seats were worn, footrests creaked or jammed, and my expectations of French elegance were dashed. I ordered a croissant, having read about these flakey delights in French grammar books and novels, but it was served cold from a fridge, soggy and fatty. A large number of the passengers were French Matelots from Tahiti, strong nuggety sailors – to a man decked out in gaudy tropical shirts. I tried making conversation with one of them who looked bemused by my correct grammar book French and promptly went to sleep.

But I was far too excited to sleep. The flight lasted for 27 hours, pacing a sun that never set. Like a magic carpet, the plane launched itself into the skies, skidding down to land in a series of enchanted places. This was 1968, when travel was such an adventure that people in Perth would go to the airport just to see a plane take off and to dream about distant countries. We landed in Cambodia, where the airport was a thatched building in a jungle clearing. Small soldiers in green camouflage trained machine guns on us as we traversed a rickety wooden platform from the plane. Sri Lanka – then called Ceylon – was dripping with humidity, and the small wooden airport building was a treasure house of jewellery for sale on rustic tables. Entranced, I bought Mother a pair of earrings like flowers, with pink stones for petals, and re-boarded the magic carpet. We landed in Athens, where my heart yearned towards tiny distant white buildings, and I bought a woven greek bag as a souvenir. Damascus was overflown, and I almost wept in frustration to think of souks and St Paul and all that we were missing.

Finally, tired to the point of hallucination, we arrived in Paris, the ultimate in imagined glamour. The airport was Le Bourget – grey, brown and dowdy, with weather to match. I was met by Madame Ladomirska, chaperone and cicerone of the group of young Australian college leavers on their Grand Tour. She was a gaunt, spare woman dressed in neutral colours, and wearing sensible flat shoes, despite which she emanated an air of European chic. Her expression was determined but behind her spectacles there was a hint of humour and sharp intelligence. We went on an astonishing metro journey to a "Centre de Jeunesse", a brutalist concrete structure where students were housed in dormitory accommodation. Paris, it seemed, was not the confection of pink towers and turrets tipped with gold that I had imagined.

After 27 hours of excited wakefulness on the plane it was hard to see straight, but Madame Ladomirska piloted me to my first French Restaurant – a workman's cafe in an adjoining street where we ate creamy omelettes, more delicious than any concoction made of eggs that I had ever tasted. She explained, "For good food, go where the workmen go." Lesson No 1.

Mme Ladomirska, or Mrs Lado as we came to call her, was a redoubtable Dutch woman who had lived in Australia and used her multilingualism to teach at one of the many private colleges in my home town, Perth. She came from a Dutch family living in Java. Her language career had begun when she was taken at a young age to Europe as a member of an Indonesian Gamelan band. That experience, as a small member of the orchestra with its gongs, chimes and bells, taught her to love travelling. She was subsequently sent by her parents to Paris to learn French, but, with an eye for a bargain she was boarded with a German family so that she could learn the two languages at once. She seemed to have survived the ensuing mental confusion and later picked up native speaker English, capping it all by acquiring a Polish husband. Mrs Lado had a simple plan. She loved Europe and travelling, and she was a born teacher. She had evolved the idea of taking a group of young Australian women, fresh from school on a year's Grand Tour to Europe, studying French in Paris and Italian in Italy. She joined in the Italian classes herself to add one more language to her collection. She taught them – and me into the bargain – the art of travelling on a shoestring, armed with Arthur Frommer's "Europe on Five dollars a Day", and the Michelin Guide Bleu. We were taught always to look up, when we walked along streets, to see the architecture, always to look into courtyards for wells and treasures, always to read menus before going into a restaurant, to buy the cheapest transport tickets and free passes to museums and galleries, and to be on the lookout for new experiences wherever we went. And above all, to avoid speaking English whenever possible. This last, among a group of chatty 18 year old girls who had been to school together, was the most difficult. I counted myself lucky to join the group as a sort of older sister and extra chaperone. The five girls whom I met at the Centre de Jeunesse, would be the supporting cast for the next months in Europe. Tall, sweet faced Susan, witty Sue, complex and thoughtful Dido, Sylvie, bubbly and French, tiny, smiling

Shelley, and direct, tomboyish Jennifer. They would be a greek chorus of excited guides, as we shared new experiences, and would become young sisters, bringing their problems to be solved.

On the first day of the European experience, the whole group boarded a bus to go to Mont St Michel, that castle-Monastery perched on the edge of Normandy and approached over a salt marsh. We climbed the long series of steps up to the Monastery which were lined with tiny shops selling every variety of plastic Mont St Michels, spoons, dishes, key rings and monkish fluffy toys. We stopped at a tiny cafe to have a lunch of the Mont St Michel omelettes and 'pre salted lamb', from the marshes, and arrived in the massive grey stone monastery buildings. They were freezing, cavernous and empty. Wandering around, I tried to imagine the life of the Benedictine monks who had lived there. Fresh from a warm Western Australia, the sea wind felt icy and I had real sympathy for those monastic ascetics who would have risen before dawn and padded along the icy corridors to chapel in sandalled feet. How cold they must have been! Hoping for ghosts or wisps of Gregorian chant I found little until at the very heart of the monastery I came upon a small chapel that was alive with candles and glowing red votive lights. I sank gratefully onto one of the wooden benches for peace and prayer – mostly of the "I'm a bit lost, Lord" variety. The peace was brief. It was a rude contrast when we boarded the bus to return to Paris. In an atmosphere choked with cigarette smoke, a raucous voiced American woman set up excruciating jazz community singing.

On the second day in Paris, Mrs Lado announced that it was necessary to "Learn the Metro". Underground railways were new to me. We went into town and I was bought a carnet of tickets and coached on navigating the maps and the station gates. We emerged, poking our heads up into daylight like Mole from the Wind in the Willows, in the region of Le Marais. Today a thriving and fashionable area of restaurants and tourism, in 1968 it was almost deserted, full of weed-filled derelict sites and beautiful ghostly empty buildings that had been revealed after bomb and slum clearance. Now, they were awaiting resurrection. With an eye more accustomed to modern Australian architecture, I wandered around, feeling ever more lonely and desolate and wondering what it was I should be appreciating. It seemed as though Paris was full of spectres of the past and I was unable to contact them. Then I happened upon the Place des Vosges, and saw that I was standing in front of Victor Hugo's house. At last, a friendly spirit. He was a hero of mine. I had read and loved his writings. I went in and immersed myself in memorabilia and stories, emerging with a photograph of a touching statuette of "Cosette", the little waif, which I tucked into my bag to send home to Mother, who was always a sentimental Victorian romantic at heart.

Having mastered the Metro, I went early into the centre of Paris. Coming from a country where few buildings were older than 100 years, I had longed to stand on the floor of a really ancient edifice. I chose a likely looking church and went in. It looked ancient to me, the stones chipped and venerable. I stopped, trying to feel its age and sense its history. As I stood, the doors of three carved black confessional boxes sprang open like cuckoo clocks and three black robed priests emerged. I almost expected them to say "Cuckoo!" In my innocence, I was standing in St Sulpice, a church that was "modern" by European standards, being built between 1646 and 1732. It was at least before European settlers had reached Australia. I discovered much later that St Sulpicien was a term used by Parisiens to describe sentimental nineteenth century religious art. Had I realised my chronological mistake at the time it might not have bothered me too much. I emerged happy to have stood on what seemed to me to be ancient flagstones and I had seen the cuckoo clock doors of the confessionals sprung.

It was the first of many visits to Parisian churches. I would creep in, fascinated by the shadowy interiors, to kneel in silence or attend a Mass. My attitude was always one of enquiry, looking at God with my head on one side, asking where to go next, what was the next turning in the path. My constant prayer was "Please show me what you want me to do and give me the strength and courage to do it." But most of the time the only answer was a mysterious silence.

On Sunday afternoons there was a 3pm organ recital in the nave of the vast cathedral of Notre Dame. Not, in those days, a forest of jostling tourists waving iPhones, but a haven for worshippers, while any visitors tiptoed quietly down the side aisles, anxious not to make a noise. The great organ would boom out, vibrating the bones. Sometimes the concert would be played by the famous musician Cochereau. Sometimes the music would be a shimmering work by the composer Messiaen.

The first weeks in Paris were both surprising and shocking as I encountered the utter strangeness of France, made stranger because of half comprehended descriptions absorbed from French literature. Paris was not built of rose-gold stone. It did not shimmer as it did in impressionist paintings. Paris in the spring was not the lovers' delight I had been led to imagine but a grey and icy city where winds blew through my Australian coat and where my Australian shoes let in the water from seemingly permanent puddles. Cobbled and paved streets were new to my feet and after several days of walking they became painful in every bone. People were exclaiming that there were leaves on the trees – where? All I could see were bare black branches, which themselves were a strange new experience coming as I did from a country that had few if any deciduous trees.

The grammar classes at the Alliance Française proved to be dry and tedious, and the hours of classes analysing "La Peste" by Camus, seemed like pointless academic hair-splitting. I have no memory whatsoever of the famed "Cours de Civilisation" which had seemed so promising and exciting, but consoled myself with the thought that my French must be improving all the time. Despite having gained high marks in Matriculation French in Australia, I found myself so tongue tied that I walked around for three days, not daring to order food, subsisting on cups of black coffee, the only thing I felt confident enough to order. Not surprising, then, that I had the sensation of floating a foot off the ground. The days were spent walking, browsing among the books displayed by the bouquinistes along the Seine, marvelling at the literary calibre of the yellow paperbacks being read by travellers on the Metro, and the fact that every street sweeper and house-painter seemed to be au fait with the latest art exhibition.

Art exhibitions, too, were a challenge. There were so many of them and they were so massive. Initially I felt morally obliged to walk very slowly around every room, pausing to appreciate every painting until exhaustion and sore feet set in. I finally realised that a cup of coffee might solace the soul as well or better. I set off every Thursday evening to take advantage of the Louvre free opening. The illuminated Winged Victory was inspiring, but I would inevitably find myself despondently marooned among endless galleries of Egyptian spoons. Beautiful though they may have been in their vivid colours, and helpful to Egyptians in the next life, I had no particular affinity with them. One day, entering a gallery of landscapes by Italian painters, I was transfixed by the bright blue skies and my mood suddenly lifted with the realisation of what had been lacking. I had needed the sun! The paintings brought back the blue and gold landscape of home, lifting the heart from depression to joy.

I wondered at the unremitting black, beige and grey worn by Parisians and slowly realised that my Australian clothes stood out like a parrot in a flock of crows. A much-loved red coat was taken to a back street dry-cleaners to be dyed an anonymous navy blue in a vain effort to blend in. It was not a likely outcome bearing in mind my round face and blonde plait.

The spring that had been promised in April finally arrived, and patisseries and chocolateries blossomed for the public holiday Muguet Day, with its ancient French tradition of giving loved ones a sprig of Lily of the Valley to symbolise renewal and the beginning of spring. I began to enjoy the internationalism of the student world and made friends with people of differing nationalities. Saying goodbye to a Canadian classmate at the Gare du Nord, I turned away, not so much with regret, but with excited wonder at who I might meet next.

The next friends arrived en route to a pilgrimage. Father Ted Stormon, my Jesuit friend and advisor in Perth, had recommended that I should seek out the Pilgrimage to Chartres and take part in it. He had explained that it was an annual event, a walk from Paris to Chartres, based on a pilgrimage done by the French writer Charles Peguy as a form of prayer for his sick daughter. Walking around the Sorbonne I came upon the Centre Richelieu, advertising the "Pélerinage" in large posters together with dozens of trips, theatres and other delights. I went in and found that it was simple to enrol and take part. 10,000 young people would walk from Paris to Chartres over two days; 5000 on each of two consecutive weekends. It involved weekly discussion groups to prepare beforehand, on topics to be discussed en route. This seemed like a way both to improve French conversation and meet new friends. I found the cafe where the discussions were to take place and met a group of a dozen or so students already there. I noticed that whereas in English we would say "Is this seat taken?" In French the expression is "Is this seat free?" It seemed to imply a more optimistic outlook.

We were to be in the "Route Rubis" for international students who did not belong to a particular faculty of a French University. Nonetheless we were expected to undertake intellectual discussions on moral and spiritual topics in the serious fashion that I was beginning to realise was a French characteristic. After the main work of the evening was over, it was time for coffee and to form friendships with the young people with whom we would be walking. I met Beatrice, from Switzerland, a budding interpreter, and Gigliola, from Verona, who was au-pairing in Paris with a view to working in the tourism industry. We quickly became friends, swapped addresses and began a round of coffee meetings and walks.

The 4th May, the day of the pilgrimage, drew near. We hired sleeping bags, plates, tin mugs, and cutlery, and were advised to bring waterproof clothes and shoes. By this time, my feet were painful from exploring Paris's cobbled streets, and the only shoes comfortable enough more resembled slippers – it was before the days of trainers. We prepared to set off early on pilgrimage day, which was a chilly spring morning. We arrived at Gare Montparnasse, (how French to name a railway station after Mount Parnassus) and the crowds of eager and chattering students climbed aboard. French students may have known the route – I had no idea where the train would take us, or what was in store. I had committed to doing this pilgrimage in a kind of blind faith that somehow, somewhere it would lead to the spiritual goal I was seeking. Perhaps that motivation had a lot in common with the goals – or non-goals – of pilgrims down the ages, who so often find what they did not know they were looking for.

The train stopped at a rural village, all cottages and hay, and we clambered out, donned our rucksacks and began walking. The group leaders carried tall, wooden crosses bedecked with flowers. There was an hour's march, then a halt, then an hour of silence. On Swiss Beatrice's recommendation we had brought large slices of solid German rye bread, saucisson and cheese, plus chocolate, all of which which became steadily less digestible as the days wore on. We saw acres of yellow rape flowers, which lit up the landscape like a theatrical spotlight, we walked past woods and through winding stone villages, and ate picnic meals in orchards full of birdsong and pink blossom.

Rained on for what seemed an eternity, the only sound at times was the squelch of water in 600 pairs of boots and shoes. Catholic, Anglican, Orthodox, and a few mildly Atheist students discussed morality and literature. It would be interesting to recall the substance of those discussions, but all I can remember is feeling quite inadequate and staying largely silent in the endless buzz of high-minded chatter. By the time I had constructed an acceptable contribution the conversation had inevitably moved on. Freezing wet feet in time become anaesthetised, and quite easy to walk on.

We finally arrived at the Chateau d'Esclimont for the night. We were ushered into a large space in front of the floodlit baby castle, shaded by trees, all fairytale towers and turrets and moat. All 5000 students converged there, singing a traditional medieval song that harmonised along the moving lines. Everyone had a candle which we lit from flame to flame as darkness descended. Down the slope came the white-clad procession and choir vaguely flickering in strings of light. They sang as they walked, a tenor with pure clarity of voice and diction and boy sopranos of silver. All were disciplined perfectly as they sang Gelineau Psalms and Taize chants, melodious and simple enough for the enthusiastic students to repeat after one hearing. Mass was said, and it was announced that two of the pilgrims were to be baptised and received into the church. My heart almost broke with longing. This was my dearest wish, but for me it was not going to happen that night. I wondered what more I would need to do or find or discover, before this event could take place. But mindful of Ted Stormon's insight that I needed to trust and find my way, still the outsider, I could only watch the proceedings with yearning.

We were led to our sleeping quarters for the night. As a soft young suburban Australian used to comfortable beds I was shocked to discover that we were expected to curl up in our sleeping bags in a shed full of straw and decked with charrettes – ancient wooden farm carts that might have been used to transport the condemned to the guillotine during the French Revolution. By that time, too tired to think, there was no option but to follow everyone else. We made nests in the straw. In fact it was the softest and best night's sleep imaginable.

Early in the morning it was too cold to wash – the only water was in the farm drinking troughs, and cows should not drink soapy water. We set off, too numb with sleep and cold to discuss philosophy. At breakfast time we stopped in a little grey village and rather miserably ate bread and butter and ham and chocolate and drank cold Nescafe with sugar. The day repeated with marches, debates, rain, sun and silence. To stay warm the Spanish did flamenco dances, the Germans taught everyone ski-camp dances, and everyone jumped up and down singing an approximation of the Can- Can and Yi Yippee Yi.

At last came the sunset walk towards Chartres, the cathedral standing on the skyline, silhouetted in the midst of wheat fields seemingly scattered with gold dust. Our footsore lines limped in, still singing, directed by grinning gendarmes. The lofty cathedral was warm and the windows were lit by the last rays of the sun. Like tired sardines we squashed together in rows on the floor. Our exhaustion was uplifted by the choir and music from the previous night this time accompanied by the great Chartres organ and a flight of angelic golden trumpets from the monastery in Taize. The sound was overwhelmingly beautiful in our state of tiredness and achievement. Down the centre of the cathedral was a table with 100 golden chalices, each one attended by a priest in white robes. Under the bright lights, they could have been attendants of the Holy Grail in a scene from Wagner's opera Parsifal. It was a practical way of feeding the multitudes who wanted communion. After this spiritual feast we caught the train back, ravenously eating baguettes and camembert. Our long days of walking were transmuted into a train ride of an hour and a half. Gare Montparnasse was filled with limping, singing, cheering students saying goodbye and planning reunions next week.

After the cheer of the pilgrimage, Paris in May 1968 was not a relaxed place to be. For all I knew it was always like this, with tension in the air. Mrs Lado, who knew Paris well and could read between the lines in newspapers, was nervous that some kind of uprising was about to happen. She spoke to us about student unrest and clashes with the police. These ideas were so foreign to my experience that her words went over my head. On 6th May, with my friend Beatrice, I walked to the Luxembourg gardens for a peaceful sunset. There was distant shouting and quite suddenly we found ourselves in the midst of a riot. Crowds took fright and began to run, cars crawled and hooted, men climbed light poles to see better, and after a particularly panic stricken dash up the Boulevard St Michel, a few students began to tear up the iron gratings around trees and lit fires in the middle of the street. A marching battalion of armed policemen with helmets, perspex shields and batons appeared and filled the road. People scampered away, red eyed from tear gas. With uncharacteristic kindness, Parisians opened the gates to their courtyards to allow the fleeing crowds to shelter from police brutality. We eventually emerged from our safe doorways and made for the Metro. Unknown to me, this was only the beginning. I had no idea of the violent and historical events that were about to unfold.

The next day I sat at breakfast with two students from Belgium. As we ate our bread and drank our enormous bowls of cafe au lait, they issued an invitation to visit them in Louvain. The next weekend, setting off by train, I saw the countryside becoming flatter and greyer as we approached the Low Countries. Welcomed into their student accommodation I was introduced to Belgian chocolate, frites and waffles and was given a tour of Brussels with its monumental greyness and its piles of roadworks due to the installation of the new Metro. We went to Bruges and saw, somewhat bemusedly, the chapel of the Holy Blood, and to a student club where there was a lively debate going on about the rights and wrongs of the Jewish/Palestinian question. The students then might have given in to terminal depression if they had realised that fifty-five years later, the same questions would still be debated with appalling violence. Louvain, or Leuven, was entrancing with its myriad chiming clocks and the carillons in the bell towers, and I was diverted by my first sight of a nun on a bicycle. I could not have been more surprised if I had seen a dog or a rabbit pedalling along. The weekend over, I went to the station to get a train ticket back to Paris.

"There are no trains to Paris Madame," was the reply. Obviously my response was along the lines of "Don't be ridiculous, of course there are trains to Paris".

"Mais non, Madame, Il n'y a pas de trains, pas d'autobus, pas d'avions. Paris est fermé."

I retired from the booking office to reconsider, and looked at a table of newspapers. I was so taken aback at the information that I read the entire front page of a newspaper in Italian without realising what language it was written in.

The Manifestations of May 1968, a series of strikes and protests against capitalism, consumerism, American imperialism, and traditional institutions, had closed France down to the outside world. Nearly 11 million workers had joined in, society was in meltdown and the government was in danger of falling. The latest news was that the only communication network was Radio Luxembourg for urgent messages, the only transport was military lorries, there were shortages of water, gas, meat, fruit and vegetables, and petrol was running out. When cars ran out of fuel they were simply abandoned – the Place de la Concorde was crammed with empty vehicles in addition to the burnt out shells of petrol bombed cars. The Sorbonne was occupied by students; lecture rooms had become dormitories, factories had been taken over by workers. There was talk of Trade Unions and rumours of a force known as the "Katangese" becoming involved. (Later I discovered that the Belgian-trained Katangese Gendarmerie had fought in the Belgian Congo during Moise Tshombe's insurrection against President Lumumba and after 1967 many of them had come to Europe as exiles.)

The National Assembly took a vote, but did not get a sufficiently large majority to unseat the government. It was thought de Gaulle might stay long enough to make a big speech later in the week – if he didn't flee or was not assassinated first.

What to do? I was an exile from Paris. In a Brussels Librerie, I bought a map of Europe. Metaphorically sticking a fork into the map, I decided that since Paris was out of the question I may as well travel to another country.

Luxembourg was nearby, where I checked into a small hotel. The gentlemen in the bar directed some odd glances at me as I primly and innocently went to my room. It was not until the next morning that I discovered the hotel was in the middle of the red-light district. It was an inauspicious start, and – as the rest of Europe seemed to be – Luxembourg was grey and wet. Sketching the romantic castle of Vianden, north of Luxembourg, in the rain, struggling with sketch pad and umbrella, I found myself grimly muttering "Enjoy it, enjoy it, you will never be here again!"

Intending to visit Beethoven's birthplace in Bonn, I was too slow to alight and the train went on to Cologne. I felt that the Gestapo might be about to pounce since I had no ticket, but I jumped off the train nonetheless, and following Mrs Lado's advice, looked up. I saw through the glass station wall the mountainous facade of Cologne Cathedral, teeming with a thousand statues, like a wall of people bewitched and turned to stone. Later, in the hotel, I encountered a duvet for the first time and was puzzled as to whether to sleep on it, under it or in it. The hotel receptionist tried his luck and, although not exactly sure what his intentions might be, I used up most of my German in saying "Nein, Nein Hans". In Amsterdam I landed on the floor of a Dutch acquaintance called Rikje, who generously showed off the glories of her city. I revelled in Van Gogh, and Rembrandt, and the Concertgebouw, and sampled the delights of the hot food for sale in glass fronted street machines – mostly some kind of unidentifiable prime matter fried in breadcrumbs.

Finally, according to newspapers, it seemed that the borders of France were open. To be safe, rather than depending on trains I caught a KLM flight back to Paris on 11th June.

Paris was unrecognisable. There were piles of rubbish in evidence, shops were boarded over, and burnt out vehicles littered the streets. Almost more uncanny was the behaviour of the Parisians. Brought together by shared adversity they were actually talking to each other, empathising and being mutually helpful. The trouble seemed to be over, but revolutionaries had one last night of surprises up their sleeves. I was having coffee with Italian Gigliola near Sèvres Babylone when we noticed a suspicious quietness in the area. While cafe owners hurriedly turned out lights and put up shutters, we ran for my tiny attic apartment. Scores of busy young people were soon dragging huge cotton reels of cable to the centre of the street. The Rue de Sèvres was barricaded. Suddenly tear gas, Molotov cocktails and grenades filled the air. Flames ran down the street gutters, setting the barricades, and some police cars, on fire. All night the explosions came from every corner of Paris and flashes lit the sky. The rioters tried to set a fire below our balcony, but mercifully someone pointed out that it was a cul de sac and they would be trapped. We settled down to try and sleep, our eyes streaming from the tear gas which was caught under the mansarde roof.

The next morning people were out picking up glass and looking at sad burnt-out car shells. Shop assistants were clearing the debris from the doorways and cleaning soot from the windows. De Gaulle, having left the country, returned. An edict was issued forbidding any further manifestations, and promising to imprison any group that gathered. Any foreign student in a riot would be deported.

And that, apart from political manoeuvring and a gigantic clean-up operation, was that.

The time in Paris was approaching its final days. The study courses had all closed down but we had gained some unexpected revolutionary vocabulary and phrases. With a mixture of regret and relief I packed up books and goods, and planned to take a train to Italy for the next bout of studies, hoping that there would be no rioting in Italy, that the

Università per Stranieri in Perugia would not close down, and that life would be calmer from now on. No one could have predicted that for me at least, life was about to get a good deal more complicated in ways I had never planned or expected.

3
BELLA ITALIA

Laden with suitcase, now heavy with books and papers, I set off for Italy, via Switzerland, in July 1968. Fortunately Aunt Ruby's awful travelling wardrobe had been disposed of along the way, explained as a casualty of the revolution. As always I only had a vague idea of what I might see, based on books and imagination. I was transfixed when the alps hove into view. Nothing could have prepared me for their towering beauty and their brutal size. Snowy peaks, cows, green slopes and even mountain streams frothing along by the railway lines. Switzerland seemed like a moving travel brochure. Travel by train was a ticket to a living technicolored movie flashing past the windows.

On arrival Switzerland looked – well – Swiss, with white houses, pointed roofs and red geraniums. I was whisked to my friend Beatrice's house where I became acquainted with the Swiss penchants for eating birchermuesli at any time of the day or night, and departing en masse at weekends to climb a mountain – always wearing stout boots and knitted red socks. I was introduced to the delights of Fondue, Swiss chocolate, and to the joy of sitting on a handy mountainside, eating ice-cream and listening to church clocks chiming.

A few days later, the departure from Zurich to Italy had several false starts. I went to the station to find there was a train strike in Italy, so I went home. On the second attempt the conductor said he didn't know whether the strike was over or not, and the train might only go as far as Chiasso. I threw my luggage off and leapt out bodily – at least there was a chance of one more evening of raspberries and cream on a hill overlooking Zurich, with lights and a lake.

Once safely on the train the next morning, the Alps continued to astound. As we approached Milan the houses became less tidy and Geranium-decked. They gave the impression of having been shifted by a careless housekeeper and left slightly askew, their red roofs facing each other at haphazard angles.

The train pulled into Milan Stazione Centrale. I put my head out of the window and felt an unaccustomed blast of joie de vivre. People seemed to be running in all directions, throwing luggage onto trolleys, yelling happy and dramatic instructions to each other against the background of a cacophony of vendors shouting- "Acqua Pellegrino Acqua!" I didn't know what that was, but it was in beautiful green glass bottles and I resolved to try it as soon as possible. Perhaps it was some kind of magic elixir since it seemed to bring such joy.

From Milan to Florence the train was crowded. I learned that the concept of a queue is unknown to Italian travellers. It was a case of 'survival of the fittest' to climb into the train. Despite my technique of placing the suitcase diagonally across the doorway and vaulting over it to foil pushy competitors, I found myself not in a compartment, but in the end space of a carriage – shared with nine men, eleven suitcases, two parcels and anyone who had drunk too much of the magic elixir Pellegrino and was now falling over us in haste to reach the very smelly Gabinetto. The Tuscan countryside was glimpsed through an impressionist haze of cigarette smoke and a very small window. We continually bobbed into tunnels at critical moments and emerged into a completely different landscape as though someone had torn a page out of a book. The scenery we glimpsed was beautiful and tantalising but it was rather like watching a jerky am-

ateur film, seen sporadically in conditions of acute and
malodorous discomfort.

At Florence there were several hours to wait before the
train for Perugia. Stowing my luggage in the "Deposito" I
walked towards the white, green and pink marble-striped,
Duomo. Outside it was all pictures, statues and pigeons and
inside, crowded and bustling with tourists. At last I was surrounded by the romantic pink, green and golden buildings
of my dreams. Rounding a corner, Ghiberti's bronze doors
were there glowing and alive. There was a cluster of ad-
mirers around the doors, looking up in ecstasy as they drank
in the panels filled with delicate soft movement. We seemed
to be getting wet, something was dripping down on us. An
American voice exclaimed in my ear, "My Gahd, it's bur-
rds!" And it was!

Having wiped the bird mess from my sleeve, I bought a
paper bag of grapes and walked around the Duomo eating
them. I found the Piazza dei Signori with Michelangelo and
Donatello statues in the square and gazed longingly at the
Palazzo Vecchio, looking as it does like the ancient ar-
chetypal castle from a legend. Peeping into the painted,
pillared and fountained courtyard I reluctantly resisted the
temptation to climb the tower and see Firenze from the top
battlements. By this time the train was nearly due to leave –
though it would hardly have mattered since I was almost
levitating with joy and could have flown to Perugia unaided.

After Firenze, came Arezzo, Terontola – then Perugia. At
least that was the plan. Between Florence and Terontola a
man fell off the train. All the workmen in the carriage enjoyed the diversion immensely. The train stopped and the
ground was covered with running, gesticulating Italian men
in overalls. They came back some time later and clambered
back in saying, with some disappointment, "No-one is
dead!"

By this time we had of course missed the connection to Perugia. On the next leg of the journey one of the wheels began to smoke dangerously. Once again the train ground to a halt. This time, rather than men in overalls, a very small but exquisitely braided and uniformed guard jumped out and ran to extinguish any flames, carrying what must have been the tiniest toy fire extinguisher ever invented. Once more there was a babble of excitement as we waited by the lines for the drama to be over, looking at the red poppies growing between the tracks.

Finally the train arrived into Perugia Statione Centrale at dusk. We looked up at a fairy-tale town, pink and golden in the sunset, illuminated with lights. The bus laboured up the hill through ramparts and palaces and churches. At one moment, out of the corner of my eye, a vignette of the Madonna appeared through an arched church door. There she stood, with neon stars whizzing around her head in electric benediction and rays of light zig zagging from her palms. We swooped around hairpin curves overlooking immense panoramic views of church towers, hills and vineyards. It was hard to believe that it was real and not a larger than life film set that might be dismantled or disappear magically at sunrise.

I was deposited at the Via della Gabbia, and the six Australian girls tumbled out like a litter of welcoming puppies, with Mrs Lado a dignified presence behind. They had arrived a week earlier and were keen to share their discoveries. Our Pensione was an apartment up uneven stone stairs into a warren of rooms filled with old furniture that might one day become antiques if it lasted long enough. There was one shared bathroom with unreliable plumbing and a kitchen barely wide enough to turn round in, where the plump, loud and jolly Signora Mercouri Ridolfi cooked substantial meals on a tower of pots, balanced precariously one on top of the other. The Signora talked constantly, which was good for our Italian, keeping up a refrain of "Mangi Signorina, mangi" ("Eat Signorina eat!") as she piled food onto plates.

The next morning dawned sunny and warm and after a breakfast of crusty rolls and coffee we set off for the Università per Stranieri. There was something about the energy in the air, the sunlight and the cheerful noisiness in the street that lifted the spirits and almost raised one off the ground. Just as I had felt in Florence, I could have soared above the city.

We skimmed over uneven cobbles, wove through pigeons and under vaulted arches and down a steep street where people were tossing back tiny cups of fragrant coffee on the way to work and ironmongers were already hammering their intricate lamp stands and furniture in tiny dark alleys. Passing arches, vaults, steps, tunnels, ancient wells and caverns, we emerged into the light at the bottom of the street. Through the gigantic Etruscan Arch with its monstrous brutal abutments, the University faced us, the Renaissance Palazzo Gallenga, full of students, marble staircases and lecture rooms hung with huge glittering Venetian glass chandeliers.

With eyes out on stalks I enrolled with a secretary who sat at a vast gilded renaissance desk and went to sit an entry test. This placed me in "Medio", the medium level of difficulty, a class presided over by Signorina Amalia Visconti, a plump and elegantly dressed young woman with voluminous curly black hair. She taught in traditional grammatical style and had a trenchant wit which could be intimidating. The other Australian girls were in the Preparatorio class, taught by Dottore Baratti – far from cheap as his name implied but a master of the Direct Method, taught in the most dramatic way. A small man, he had perfected a dramatic strutting manner of teaching, up and down the raised dais, repeating phrases a thousand ways with hand gestures and drawing speech out of the most reluctant class members.

"Io," pointing to himself, "Sono Dottore Baratti."

"Tu," – pointing to the class who chorused their names.

He danced through classes, gradually constructing sentences word by word so that at the end even the most dense student emerged with phrases in his or her head. We were exhorted to talk to everyone, to go and take coffee in the bar and above all, his constant recommendation, to promenade on the Corso Vanucci "Andare su e giù, su e giù, signori, signorine!" ("Going up and down, up and down, ladies and gentlemen!")

We all left feeling a little better for his energy and enthusiasm as he stepped down, wiping his perspiring brow with a large red handkerchief. Needless to say there was a constant trickle of more senior students from more boring classes to witness these dramatic tours de force.

On the first evening I went out of the Pensione into the Piazza IV Novembre to look at the famous 13th century fountain. Standing with my back to the Duomo among the pigeons I looked down at a heart stopping sight: crowds milling about in the Corso Vanucci. Was this yet another demonstration or a riot in the making? Did I bring insurrection wherever I travelled? A closer look revealed otherwise. It was merely the fulfilment of Dottore Baratti's recommendation. People were out on 'passeggiata,' in their best clothes, promenading su e giù on the Corso Vanucci. Young people eyeing each other up and down, parents and grandparents discreetly chaperoning, groups of young men lounging on the corners remarking on every pretty girl that passed, only to be dismissed with a flirtatious toss of the head. And everywhere at tables on the pavement customers were sipping delicious looking red iced drinks – Campari Soda, which I longed to try just as soon as possible.

July passed in a fever of delight, sunshine and excitement. Going to sleep every night was just the prelude to another wonder-filled, sunny day with more laughter, more people to meet, more ice creams to try, more churches to explore, more paintings to see, more hill towns to visit. It seemed as though the girls and I laughed all day, breathless with pleasure and the effort to progress in Italian. Life was noisy and exciting, even late in the evening when children played in the street while their parent and grandparents promenaded and talked.

Every morning was a new beginning. At 6 am bells, yells and builders began simultaneously. Above us a large gentleman produced some ingenious thumps, and from the restaurant downstairs the day's quota of crashing crockery and cantatas began. The cheese shop in the stairwell opened up, sending aloft its incense of dubious fragrance. From the tiny frescoed church of St Agatha opposite our bedroom window, a cracked and cacophonous bell announced morning Mass. Sometimes I tumbled out of bed to attend, accompanied by sundry devout workers and stooped, black clad widows. An easy way to brush up the language since there was a fair chance that if the words were not familiar, the readings might be.

Then breakfast with the Signora – bread and butter, all of it saltless since 1540 when the populace of Perugia had rebelled against a salt tax imposed by Pope Paul III. Although that particular Pope is long gone, the rebellion and the saltless bread remain as a proud warning of just what Perugini citizens can do if they really try.

Scampering down the paved streets to the University was always an adventure, dodging small carts, and vespas ridden by youths who regarded it as a challenge to ride their machines up stone staircases or thump them down to the imminent peril of passers-by. The only downside of these walks were those groups of young men I had seen at the passeggiata hour, whose sole occupation in life seemed to be lounging at corners, ogling all the girls as they passed. Known as "Pappagalli", which translates as parrots, they did indeed dress very colourfully in suits that ranged from terracotta to pumpkin orange, paired with bright shirts and ties, very bright socks and elegant Italian shoes. They had a fine line in "Psst" for pretty girls, were said to pinch on occasion and sometimes came up with a witticism such as "Hey bionda! E naturale o una perucca?" ("Hey blondie! Is that natural or a wig?") Having gone through various grades of irritation, it finally dawned that this was a kind of national sport, best ignored or laughed off. The gaudy young blades never seemed to do anything worse than strut and shout, although the wittiest of the Australian girls, Sue, unwise enough to engage in conversation did conclude that Italian young men only had three settings – "Warm, hot and Basta!" (Enough!) I would experience this for myself.

After a concentrated and hot morning in lecture theatres we would haul ourselves back up the hill for one of the Signora's three-course lunches, made from fresh produce bought at the market and miraculously concocted over her tiny gas stove. After her preliminary shout of "Mangi Signorine", we would be silenced with mounds of pasta, followed by a secondo of meat and vegetables. If anyone made feeble protests, the Signora would just say "Perché?", (Why?) and continue ladling. Further protests would call forth her coup de grace: "In Italia le ragazze più grasse sono più belle!" (In Italy the fatter girls are the most beautiful!) and that would be that.

After lunch came the official hour of siesta but the cooing pigeons didn't know this and neither, it seemed, did Signora who washed up joyously, using the plates as cymbals, and entertained anyone who came in for a chat or a visit.

Baths in the small bathroom with its scum-ringed iron bath and dubious plumbing were strictly rationed to twice a week per guest. This was due to the water system of Perugia which was associated with a medieval Aqueduct built in1254. In actual fact it had not operated since the end of the 19th century, being replaced by a complicated system of lead pipes but this did not deter the Signora. Whenever there was a problem with the water supply a shout would go up: "L'Aquedotto è rotto" (the Aqueduct is broken), and that would be the end of the matter. Washing up, flushing toilets and above all baths would be vetoed until the problem was fixed. When the water came back there would be shouts of triumph, and various guests would be seen creeping to the bathroom for their rare soak, carrying an Italian towel as thin as a tea cloth, soap, and the vital flat plug to deputise for the one provided which always let the water out, leaving the bather stranded like a deflated hippopotamus. And as we crept across the kitchen on the way to the bathroom, hoping not to be noticed, we would always be wished, in stentorian tones, "Buon bagno!" – "Have a good bath!"

Life was never dull at No 5 Via della Gabbia (Street of the Cage). True, we no longer had the medieval iron cage that was once suspended above the street to house miscreants until they were reduced to skeletons. Nor did we have the "doors of death", square passages once used for the entry and exit of coffins (lest death should enter into the house by the main door) which had run along the Via dei Priori below our windows and were now bricked up. We did, however, have washing lines that stretched along the buildings so that laundry could be pegged outside the window. This worked well until the neighbours also wanted to hang out their washing and reeled the line along so that our precious underwear rapidly progressed towards the furthest corner of the street. Even worse, sometimes the pegs would give way and one would look out to see a curious Italian gentleman poking at some intimate garment with his walking stick. This would prompt a mad rush down the stone stairs to snatch up the offending object with an embarrassed "Scusi Signor!"

We were also diverted by the other occupants of the house. The Signora's small husband crept out from underfoot at every opportunity, to sit at the corner cafe discussing who knows what mysterious 'business' with his friends, occasionally reappearing with some 'masterpiece' he had bought at an art exhibition. Her plump son was doted on and cherished, while her thin daughter was constantly shouted at to do chores. And there were three medical students who inhabited rooms on another floor and came in for coffee from time to time. One of them, Mimmo from Abruzzo, took it on himself to take me for evening walks to view the sunset and improve my mastery of Italian. He seemed to be quiet and gentlemanly until one evening when he made a pounce and suddenly wasn't. I fled, and never spoke to him again. I was not looking for a relationship. Certainly not one that involved unwanted sexual advances. Nothing could have been further from my mind. Life was about travel, language learning, art and culture.

Sometimes there was a concert in one of the many churches. One night there was a piano recital upstairs in the Palazzo Dei Priori. Opening velvet curtains with a swish we found ourselves in a large vaulted hall lined with priceless Umbrian paintings. The piano recital commenced and I found my eyes wandering over the pictures, transfixed by a depiction of the unfortunate local patron Saint Ercolano, looking very pink and naked and carrying his skin over one arm, as though he had taken it off and was going for a shower. Poor Bishop Ercolano. He had a terrible end, being flayed, beheaded and thrown from the city walls in retribution for leading the defence of Perugia against the attack of Totila the Ostrogoth. They were cruel times. Perhaps the picture was meant to encourage the viewer to aim for martyrdom but the effect was precisely the opposite.

But the most exciting incident was the "Night of the Mouse". Dido, one of the girls, felt it sitting on her in bed. She shot upright, and the Signora was informed. Signora was firmly sceptical at first, on the illogical grounds that there had never been one before. However, il topo mistakenly ran past her into the kitchen. She slammed the door shut, put three chairs against it so il topo couldn't open it for himself, and ran to fetch help from the neighbours. We then listened to something very like the last act of Tosca, as three Italians united in the effort to murder one small rodent in the tiny kitchen. From the sound of the shouting and the banging it seemed likely that they would do more damage to each other than to the tiny creature in such a small space. When silence descended, we assumed that poor Mr Mouse had been dispatched. However, from that day things were dated as "Before Mouse" and "After Mouse", since the Italian for the latter came out nicely as "Dopo il topo".

4
BROWN EYES

It was the brown eyes that did it. Dark brown eyes that were warm and filled with laughter, snapping with vivid life, penetrating but at times seemingly looking into the distance.

He was a tall, energetic, black-haired young man who bounced slightly when he walked and seemed to laugh more than most. He wore an open necked white shirt, grey trousers and sandals. Every morning he would come into the Aula Magna, our lofty lecture hall, laughing and chatting with his American friend who had film star looks. And yet it was the brown-eyed man, rather than his handsome friend, who constantly drew my eyes.

I discovered that the American was an evangelical missionary who was learning Italian with a view to converting the population. "Good luck with that," I thought, and imagined him knocking on the doors of houses and being ushered into rooms bedecked with rosary beads and statues of the Sacred Heart. I assumed my brown-eyed young man was part of the team and mentally christened him "The Evangelical Missionary with the far-seeing eyes." For a week or two, my eyes continued to swing in his direction when he entered the room or stood at the back, talking to his friend, before the morning "Medio" grammar lesson.

One evening an Ecumenical Service was organised to bring the international students of all religions and cultures together. We congregated on the sweeping steps of the enchanting little rotunda church of St Ercolano. The kindly and jolly students' chaplain Don Elio Bromuri officiated. The handsome American was there, as was "my" Evangelical Missionary with the "far seeing eyes" – except that this time he was dressed in full Roman priestly attire – black suit and white dog collar. It made him all the more interesting. Was this the priest I had been waiting for? Might this be someone I could talk to? My Jesuit friend Ted Stormon had sent me on a pilgrimage to find my way. Perhaps this young priest might be the contact I needed. I felt hope and filed the information away.

The next weekend, Mrs Lado organised a visit to Assisi with the girls. As usual we set off on the earliest train. We began our pilgrimage at the lowest level of the town and I was horrified to find that the tiny ancient Porziuncula, site of the earliest meetings of the friars, with its smoke blackened walls, was now overwhelmed by a monstrous marble baroque cathedral which encompassed and dwarfed it. What would St Francis, il Poverino, have said?

We trudged up to the town into the vast Cathedral with its Frescos by Giotto and Cimabue, into the Basilica of St Clare, where we were fascinated and horrified by her poor little mummified body. To anyone who had been entranced by the story of Clare, the young woman who renounced her wealth and followed Francis of Assisi into a life of poverty, this seemed a travesty. Certainly only by some stretch of the imagination could she be said to be "preserved." But nevertheless Assisi worked its magic. The high walls, geranium-lined, cast cool shadows and created silent shady tunnels which absorbed noise, no matter how many chattering visitors walked along.

We found a pasta lunch, and browsed the bookshops and stalls. I bought two copies of a favourite book, the "Fioretti" or "Little Flowers of St Francis". One was in French and one was in Italian. Ever the optimist, my ambition was to read them in tandem, cross-translating. We returned to Perugia in the early evening, hot, sweaty, tired and happy.

The next morning, as always in magical Perugia, dawned coffee-scented, sunny and blue. Like the eye of heaven, a clear sky awaited, the colour of cornflowers, bluebells, larkspurs, and delphiniums. I walked down the hill to the University and for once, resolved to bag one of the soft blue velvet armchairs in the front few rows of the Aula Magna. Before the first grammar class I crept in and placed my two paperbacks of the "Little Flowers" on a seat just to the left of the middle in the front row.

When I returned someone was sitting next to the books. It was the missionary with the far-seeing eyes, no longer in his priestly attire but back in white shirt and sandals.

We nodded. I sat down. "Buon Giorno Signorina," he said. "Buon Giorno", I replied. We looked at each other and said simultaneously in Italian, "Where are you from?" Ireland and Australia, came the reply. We began talking. In English. His name, he said, was Kieran.

Our talking continued in the break between classes. Instead of going for a coffee we leaned on the windowsill overlooking the massive Etruscan Arch and the winding Aqueduct road and swapped stories. I learned that he was indeed a missionary, but a catholic one, in Zululand. I didn't admit that I had very little idea where that was and wondered where I could find a map. He was a priest and member of the "Servi di Maria" or Servites, a monastic order founded in the 13th century by seven noblemen near Florence, who saw the need for spiritual change in their society. Temporarily working at the church of San Marcello, the head house of the Servite Order in Rome, he was helping to prepare for an important General Chapter – a meeting in which the entire constitution of the order would be reformed. Rome in the heat of August is far from ideal. Many Romans go on holiday to escape the stifling heat and everything slows down. Kieran had asked if he could do a summer course in Italian. He had decided on the Universita per Stranieri in

Perugia. Neither of us had any idea how that decision would influence and change our lives.

As the hot summer days passed, we found ourselves searching each other out between classes, and leaning out of the window of the palazzo to talk, hoping to catch a cool breeze. As we gazed out on the gigantic arch and the aqueduct, I heard about his love of the people and language of Zululand, the beauty of the hills, and "libantu bahle" – the golden hour of evening when "the people are beautiful". I heard of his delight in the chubby Zulu children carried on their mothers' backs and tumbling about like adorable puppies. I heard about Zulu singing in natural harmonies and his joy at joining in Zulu dancing. He was always so happy that he received the Zulu nickname O Nhleghayo – the Laughing one. His love of the people went along with a passionate sense of injustice at the apartheid system. He was fired with a burning desire to fight and if necessary to go to prison in the struggle for freedom.

I heard about his studies and his languages and his family in Ireland, and about his struggles with a superior who had responded badly to his criticism of the way a local order of nuns was being organised. Telling me of this, his voice quavered and I saw how deeply he was hurt to have been rebuked for standing up to what he felt were moral principles.

We talked, too, about our backgrounds. I told him about my safe suburban Australian schooldays in the sun. He told me the heartbreaking story of his childhood in post-Independence Ireland. He was the fourth of five children, three girls and two boys, and his arrival as the first son had been greeted with joy. He had a close and loving relationship with his mother, but when he was six, she developed Tuberculosis and died. For the next two years his eldest sister, Eileen, became a little mother to them all. Then further tragedy struck. Aged fourteen, on Christmas day in 1943, Eileen developed Meningitis, and died within a few days. Kieran's voice cracked as he told me how his father had cradled the dying Eileen in his arms and wept. After Eileen's funeral, his father was so overcome with grief that the house was closed down and the children put into orphanages, the girls placed in one children's home, and the boys sent to another. Kieran spoke about a sadistic matron who scrubbed their chilblains until they bled. It had made him vow that he would always be kind to children.

Eventually, life improved when he and his younger brother were sent to a Gaelic speaking college to learn the language. It would be the first of his seven languages. His eyes brightened as he told me about the kindness of the teachers there, and the story-telling sessions by the fire at night. His little brother Joe one day remarked "This must be what happy feels like". One day their father visited with a lady. They were not introduced, but when the boys returned home they found she was now their stepmother. From then on life was stable, but from the sound of his stories, conditions were still hard.

I was moved by the contrast with the predictable safety of my childhood in Perth where, in retrospect, the sun never seemed to stop shining. I told Kieran about the hot hot summers when our arms stuck to the school desks and the surprisingly cold and wet winters when the joy of an open fire and Vegemite sandwiches greeted us on our return from school. Winter evenings were spent doing homework, or playing card games beneath the standard lamp, and perhaps as a special treat making toast before bed with a long wire toasting fork in front of the dying fire. Winter days were sunny and warm, and nights gave the special pleasure of listening to rain on the red tiled roof, feeling safe and secure.

From the beginning, Kieran and I dived in deep in our conversations. One of the earliest things he said was, "I can't wait to die! I am so looking forward to meeting Jesus and taking his hand".

It was not a chat-up line. Most young women would have run a mile. As it was I was struck with awe and joy to have met someone of such open, transparent and fearless faith. I wanted to know more.

As the conversation moved on I told him about my pilgrimage to find the right time and place to be received into the Church and the years of conversations with Father Ted Stormon. Had I found my priest? Taking a deep breath I asked if he would receive me into the Church. He was initially hesitant since, as a traveller, I would not have a supportive community. He promised to think about it.

We looked forward to seeing each other. In unspoken agreement our eyes would meet and we would seek each other out, going for walks after classes or after the afternoon siesta, sitting on warm walls and discussing the world, the church, spirituality and humanity, prayer and stories and jokes mixed equally in the conversations.

We went to a small bar at Porta Pesa where he often went for a drink after an evening of study. It was run by Franco Ragni, the amiable proprietor and his smiling young American wife. Crammed into the bar, the local young men who were his friends were coaching him for his first sermon in Italian. Sunday dawned and they all turned up in the church. Kieran ascended into the pulpit. He hesitated a moment before beginning and a shout went up from his supporters at the back – "Coraggio Padre!"

I knew I enjoyed his stories, his humour and his company, but one day I saw him sitting on a wall in conversation with a beautiful blonde Scandinavian student in an open-air counselling session and felt a sense of proprietorship, which I couldn't quite explain. After all, he was just a delightful friend, and a priest at that. Had he been anything else I would not have approached him.

One morning in July he was up in arms about the new Papal Encyclical "Humanae Vitae," a pronouncement condemning artificial birth control, explaining all the reasons the Encyclical's logic was wrong. In August he was standing (literally) on a soapbox in the entrance hall of the University, addressing a small crowd about the Russian tanks that had rolled into Czechoslovakia. He was all for going there to fight. His energy, enthusiasm, warmth and charisma were evident and drew people to him.

On 16th August, something called the "Palio" was due to take place in Siena. There were posters up in the University and there was an air of excitement. Everyone, it seemed, was going. I had little idea what it was – some kind of horse race? In the middle of a town? It was hard to imagine. Father Kieran with the far-seeing eyes was going to Siena ahead of time, to stay in the monastery belonging to his Order, the Servites. We arranged to meet up in Siena at 12 o'clock on the day of the Palio.

At 5.30 am the six Australian girls and I went out to catch the bus for Siena just across the Piazza from the via della Gabbia. The Signora had packed us enormous lunches the night before and we staggered out feeling like Dick Whittingtons with our huge pink plastic-wrapped parcels.

On the way to Siena the Umbrian countryside revealed itself as the sun rose, highlighting pine-scattered hillsides and white buildings with red roofs and romantic piled up hill towns fading into misty perspective. Siena emerged with its pink walls running down the sides of hills, its towers and battlements. It seemed even more fairy-tale-like than other hill towns. From the bus park we snaked through high-sided streets as the shops opened and tables were set on the pavement, with stalls selling sweets, and fazzoletti – scarves for supporters of the "Contrade", the competing districts of the town, all in a state of frenzied patriotism exactly like football supporters in advance of a match. We emerged into the light to find ourselves looking down into the famous fan-shaped Piazza del Campo, surrounded by thirteenth century buildings decked with gold and with velvet banners hanging from the balconies. I would not have been surprised to see ladies in tall pointed hats and veils leaning over to their serenading lovers. What we did see was a piazza bustling with stallholders selling food and scarves and balloons in the colours of the contrade, and the air was noisy with the sound of "fowls" – little machines that cackled loudly when the handle was wound, adding to the gaiety of the day.

The girls and I walked and walked, inspecting streets and churches, paintings, inlaid floors and marble courtyards. We even found a church containing the head of St Catherine of Siena, though I could have sworn she had another one when we had seen her body in Rome. When we were exhausted and footsore we sat on the Fonte Gaia, the Joyous Fountain (Oh well named!), to open our lunch packs and explore the feast of bread and cheese and ham provided by our Signora.

Crowds were beginning to enter the fan shaped piazza. Citizens were decked out in Renaissance costumes, silks and velvets and parti-coloured tights, the men having grown their hair long so that it could be dressed in period style.

Father Kieran joined us and the girls melted away to investigate more stalls and gelati. I was taken on a long walk, keeping up with his rangy uneven stride, to see his monastery where from the kitchen garden there was a panoramic view over the countryside. My escort pointed out the way to the 'Little girls' room' for which I was grateful, but obscurely felt he should not be aware of such biological necessities –

rather forgetting that even priests had families and probably sisters.

He escorted me to a richly decorated chapel where he had been asked to take part in the blessing of the "Montone" or Ram district horse, prior to the race. The highly strung animal was led into the chapel dressed in gilded trappings and a velvet saddle, looking as though it had just that minute stepped out of a painting by Benozzo Gozzoli. At a vital stage of the blessing the horse stood on the jockey's foot which was hailed as a sign of good luck and Father Kieran blessed him and sent him off with the bidding: "Vai cavallo e retourni vincitor". ("Go, horse and return victorious").

At the same moment the same blessing was being intoned, for fairness, over the steeds of all other districts, so that the goose, bear, tower, unicorn and giraffe would all compete with equal divine favour.

We walked back together down the hill in the heat just in time for the procession to begin. A band of drums and long glittering trumpets led the way, followed by page boys and teamsmen tossing long pennants high into the air and catching them as they marched. Horses draped in red velvet were ridden by men in chain mail or armour, soldiers carried pikes and mediaeval weapons. Crowds of people leaned over balconies and were ranged in stands, as colourful as peacocks in their Renaissance dress. King Arthur's time seemed to have come alive again. The Palio itself, a silk banner, was borne aloft an ox cart drawn by three white beasts, accompanied by town dignitaries straight from a Renaissance portrait gallery.

We found a position at the far back of the fan shaped piazza. When the race began the excitement reached fever pitch. Horses, ridden bareback, careered round the piazza, taking corners at breakneck speed, narrowly missing dangerous stone walls padded with blankets. Some lost their riders and streaked past riderless, caught up in the pure excitement of running. Fortunately we were too distant to witness any injuries of which there must have been some. Word spread that the Goose Contrada horse had won, followed by rumours of foul play which would be hotly disputed in rival Contrade restaurants until late into the night.

The crowds were so tightly packed that it was hard to breathe. Jokes were bandied about, saying that if someone died in the crush they would not be able to fall down. As the excitement subsided, we found ourselves being propelled forcibly towards the narrow exit from the Piazza like toothpaste being squeezed out of a tube. I felt Father Kieran's arm gently and firmly around me as he sheltered me from the buffeting. My heart dropped like a stone as my whole body awoke to the sudden realisation that I loved this man, and I knew from his warm touch that he loved me too. This was my priest, and we loved each other. It was a mixture of powerful joy, ecstasy, jubilation and terror as I realised that we stood on the edge of an age old breaking of vows, of Heloise and Abelard, the opposing forces of passion and impossibility.

I looked up and made some remark like "Careful – What's this?" And in response he just squeezed my shoulders tighter.

Never will I forget the raging turmoil of emotions as Kieran, my friend, my priest and my impossible love, escorted me to the bus and stood there as I departed, watching the pink towers of Siena turn red in the sunset.

5
AN APPLE ORCHARD AND AN ANGEL

After a day or two Kieran returned from Siena. We went for a walk and sat in an old orchard behind the Monastery of Santa Maria Nuova. It was one of those summer days when Perugia decided to show what it could do in the way of storms. The skies darkened and opened, sending water-spouts gushing down the narrow paved streets and stair-ways. We dashed for cover into the Monastery. Kieran dis-appeared into his room and emerged with a gift – an Irish tea towel inscribed with an Irish blessing. I had never been presented with a tea towel before and tried not to smile. "May the road rise to meet you, may the wind be always at your back…" I was touched, it was the best he had to give. It was from the heart.

We continued our walks and talks, at ever greater intens-ity. After the evening meal with the bustling Signora I would slip out and meet Kieran sitting on the stone steps of the Palazzo dei Priori beneath the gigantic lion and griffon. We would set off amid the other couples on their evening passeggiata. Su e giù, up the Corso Vanucci, to the Piazza Italia, to lean on the ramparts in the breeze and watch the sunset, talking all the while. One evening, as we walked along, he sang to me - 'Tula Baba', a tender Zulu lullaby.

At the same time I began to realise that, like any other group of young men, monks could have a ribald sense of humour. I was quite shocked one evening when, stopping in a smelly lookout over the city, he said-

"This isn't a pizzeria, it's a pisseria!" Surely a holy father should not say or even think such things?

I heard more about Kieran's schooldays, so contrasted with my early days in the sunshine and safety of Western Australia. Whereas I had experienced kindly and motherly nuns, he had attended a secondary college where beatings were administered for minor infringements of the rules or poor work. Fortunately he liked study and escaped the cane. But life was not easy in chilly, rainy Ireland. He and his younger brother were expected to rise early, serve as altar boys at Mass in the local church, light the fire, make their own porridge for breakfast and then ride their rickety bicycles two miles to school. They made the journey four times a day, in all weathers. When it was cold or raining they just got wet and steamed dry in class. Their new stepmother had little time for the four older children and became fully occupied with her own babies. He enjoyed school and even more, enjoyed time out of school playing handball at every opportunity, a game similar to squash but using the hand instead of a racquet. The great joy of the year was the chance to spend holidays with grandparents on a tiny eight acre farm in Roscommon. There he helped dig the turf, care for the horse, the cow, the pig and the chickens. And above all, he found a mother figure in his grandmother, a truly kind and loving woman. He described her throwing food to the chickens and quoting scripture "Eye has not seen nor ear heard the glory that God has prepared for those that love Him – chuk chuk chuk!" He never forgot her. She gave his life love and balance. At the end of school, seeking community, he was attracted to the Army or the priesthood. He chose the Servite Order which appealed to his idealism. The Order had a worldwide reach and might give him a chance for adventures in Africa.

In 1954, giving his bicycle to his young brother Joe, and furnished with new clothes and the present of a watch from his father, he set off for Benburb in Northern Ireland to begin his theological studies. Originally christened 'John' after

66

his father, on entering the monastery he took the religious name Kieran, after a fifth century saint born in Ireland, who was one of St Patrick's twelve helpers. St Kieran, like his modern-day namesake, loved animals and related to them closely – and coincidentally it was the same name as his secondary college. From then on, the name "Kieran" would become his identity and he would remain Kieran for the rest of his life.

Back in Italy 1968 was the year of the song 'Azurro' and we walked one evening from the University up the steep Via Bontempi, spontaneously dancing along as the catchy song belted out of an open window, its beat and words echoing our situation in so many ways. 'Delilah' was all the rage too, in its beautiful Italian version, about a fairytale King and Queen. We had the same sense of humour and Perugia re-sounded with our laughter. One day we realised we had been talking non-stop for more than eight hours. We shared our past histories, discussed life, the world, spirituality, psychology, and the rule of celibacy for the priesthood. It had not been a rule in the early church. St Peter had a wife. It was only made obligatory in the 11th century. Kieran saw it as something that should be optional for those who felt called to the single life, but he had taken solemn vows. He could not imagine breaking those vows. We talked about love. He surprised me by saying,

"Love isn't the opposite of hate. Love is the opposite of fear. "

Walking, we dared not hold hands in case we were seen. One evening as we said a late goodbye in the della Gabbia courtyard, I dared to place a light kiss on Kieran's cheek and he turned and ran away. The situation was overwhelming, agonising and terrifying. We were like reversing magnets, drawn together and pulled apart with equal intensity.

August passed with weekend excursions to other hill towns with Mrs Lado and the girls – to Cortona where we sat on a hillside, feeling like Robert and Elizabeth Browning and heard a shepherd piping to his flock. We went to Gubbio where we missed the procession of gigantic Ceri candles, but encountered a flock of pappagalli in mustard and terracotta suits, with flagrant cerise socks, all intent on flaunting their burgeoning masculinity to this procession of six nubile Australian girls. And in Todi, we encountered one of the more diverting aspects of Italian gabinetti – the lavatory attendant. They came in all shapes and sizes. In this case, he was a very small man wearing a gold braided cap and a magnificent jacket who bowed low as each of us entered, saying

"S'accomodi Signorina," ("Make yourself comfortable!") as he handed us each a minuscule piece of toilet paper with a flourish.

And there was Verona. For the price of a mere train ticket it was possible to travel to another region of Italy and to experience something as magical as an opera in a Roman Arena. I set out agog to see Aida, complete with camels and horse drawn chariots. The moon rose over the arena like a gigantic theatrical lamp and the Italian audience, who were word perfect, sang along when when they were not eating bread and salami or drinking red wine. To my disappointment I discovered that the reputed tomb of Juliet just might have been an embellished ancient Roman horse trough. On the way back to Perugia I was highly diverted by the carriage full of Italian food enthusiasts who energetically discussed memorable meals they had eaten in every city we passed through.

Back in Perugia, a flaming August was drawing to a close. The University population was thinning out as summer students began to return home. Kieran was being called back to his monastic headquarters in Rome to prepare for the

General Chapter or meeting, which would review all of the rules and constitutions of the Servite Order. It would take place in Spain in Majadahonda. If he was going to receive me into the church this needed to be planned. We arranged that I would come to Rome in September and the deed would be done.

I caught the bus to Rome. Halfway there, at Narni having taken too long over coffee I was summarily frog-marched out of the toilet block by an impatient bus driver saying: "Presto, presto signorina, l'autobus parte!" ("Hurry hurry signorina, the bus is leaving!") Unexpected, but I suppose he could have just left me behind.

The first sight of the Eternal City was disappointing. It seemed to consist of acres of block like buildings painted in every shade of terra cotta, from pumpkin to rust, most of them unattractive. Where were the romantic ruins? The bus deposited its passengers in the Piazza della Reppublica, a large 'circular square'. There was a large fountain where Titans grappled with ferocious crocodile-like dragons spitting jets of water. We were near the gigantic Baths of Diocletian, by the Termini Railway Station. A remarkably clean emperor, it seems. The baths were a social club for the Romans with hot and cold baths, games rooms and endless pillars and courtyards. It was beautifully ruined and semi restored, draped with weeds and drowsy cats on the warm stones.

With a happy lift of the heart I saw Kieran approaching, still in his open necked shirt and sandals. I was piloted to my hotel. It was the Albergo del Sole, the oldest existing hotel in Rome built in 1467. It apparently had not been renovated since then. The ambience was dark brown and a bit dusty, as was the small room, which had an uncomfortable bed with a thin crackly mattress, an old blotchy mirror and something approximating a bathroom with an extremely nasty and ancient odour in the drains. But on the plus side, it was next door to the Pantheon, and by standing on tiptoe

I could look out and see a fountain, one corner of the famous temple and cars whizzing around the Piazza della Rotonda.

We went into the Pantheon. We were alone there, able to appreciate the airy dimensions as we gazed up at the uniquely satisfying dome with its oculus open to the sky. It had rained and there was a puddle on the floor. We went round the corner to Giuseppe's Pizzeria, a refuge for hungry monks in mufti from San Marcello when the monastic evening meal proved just too bland and boring.

Kieran had arranged that I would be employed for two weeks on a special contract at the Servite Monastery, San Marcello, to read and translate letters from Italian, French and Spanish monasteries, type them and file them for the benefit of the Father General, a large bluff American called Father Joe Loftus who was not about to get deeply involved with these foreign languages. The only problem was that the office typewriter was an IBM Golf Ball typewriter, distracting enough in itself, with a continental keyboard. The time lost in searching for keys to peck made the job an exercise in patience. Most of the correspondence was from provincial priests with various administrative problems. I remember one holy father who was very upset that his beautiful marble altar would be discarded in favour of a modern table facing the congregation. Kieran snorted "He wants to go on saying Mass 'Arsus Populum!' ".

It was a chance to see inside the head office, or Curia of a religious order. I was curious. Admitted through the front door I was taken up in a tiny creaking gated lift by a portly portiere, who then escorted me to the office through lofty corridors lined with dark and smokey pictures of saints, clerical dignitaries and anguished crucifixions. From time to time we were passed by a monk bustling about his business – most looking refreshingly normal. I did wonder if, as in Mt Athos, even female cats were barred from the premises and if I was the first woman allowed. It was hard and concentrated work, and I saw little of Kieran during the day, discretion being the better part of valour.

Lunchtime and siesta time gave a chance for a panino and coffee, to roam the streets looking covetously at shoe shops, or to sit in a park or a cool church, since the brown dusty and malodorous hotel did not hold many charms. After work, when life in Rome had woken up, Kieran and I would meet up and go for long walks. A favourite route was piazza-hopping from San Marcello in the Corso, to St Ignacio, with its aerobatic angels and cherubs on the ceiling and its trompe l'oeil dome where square shapes seemed round and changed shape as one moved. Every corner seemed to be gilded and ornamented so that the eye grew dizzy with confusion. Then to Santa Maria Minerva, built over a temple to Minerva, and on the the Piazza Navona with its massive rushing fountains representing the continents of the Renaissance known world, the church where Act I Of Tosca was set, and the shop which claimed to sell the world's best gelati. Or we would go to the treasure-house that was San Clemente, the three-level church, its upper level built in the 12th century, all golden mosaics and mellow geometric Cosmati tiles, the next level, accessed by a staircase, a fourth century frescoed church, once a Roman house, used by clandestine Christians. A fresco of the empress Theodora had been cunningly turned into the Virgin by the judicious addition of a halo. And still further down in the earth, accessed by an even darker staircase, was an ancient Mithraic temple, used by Roman soldiers, damp and dank, with a mysteriously lit statue of the god Mithras slaughtering a bull.

We never dared to hold hands in Rome in case one of Kieran's colleagues might be passing, but sometimes, in the evenings, it seemed to be permissible when crossing a wide street. I was always laughingly put on the side of the traffic, since Kieran had a theory that no Roman motorist would ever mow down a blonde. One evening we walked up the Via Veneto, so far from our usual scene. The brilliantly illuminated designer shops, the famed and expensive prostitutes with dead, made up eyes, the Americans and the would-be international set, eating and drinking at pink-clothed tables. Expensive people in expensive clothes eyeing other expensive people who were eyeing them. The area was full of illuminated rushing fountains, fiats and Vespas. As we walked along we came upon a lost American couple who needed guidance back to the Piazza Navona. Familiar with the route we offered to take them, and linked hands as we crossed a road.

"Are you two engaged?" They asked.

"No, but we'd like to be," Kieran replied.

It was galvanising. The words went like an arrow through my being. I was astonished and moved that he had said it aloud. It was a longing neither of us had ever dared to express. But instantaneously with the joy came the heart-dropping knowledge that this could never be.

En route we briefly lost our way and mislaid the Piazza Navona. With a straight face Kieran told our bewildered American tourists that in Rome, they occasionally moved piazzas a few streets to the left or right at night. They may still be puzzling over that.

One Sunday we met mid-morning, and guided by the ever useful "Europe on $5 a Day" we took a small train to Ostia Antica. The ancient Roman port built by Tiberius was deserted, and we walked freely hand in hand in the heat, our feet treading stones rutted by ancient chariot wheels, and sat on the stone seats of the Roman Arena, with darting lizards and the occasional lazy cat. As we walked we trod on thyme and marjoram growing wild among the pavements and the aromas were released into the hot air. We found a small trattoria shaded by vines and ate a herby pasta dish provided by the benevolent padrona. For one day we were sheltered in a time slip of history, able to be ourselves, two people in love as thousands might have been before in this place.

On another Sunday, together with 44,000 other people, we boarded one of the packed Roman buses, towards the Vatican. It was a marvellous ride full of laughter, with everyone falling on top of everyone else. When the doors snapped closed a shout went up:

"Hey, C'e un pezzo fuori!" ("Hey, there's a piece of someone outside!")

When we arrived for the Sunday morning Papal Audience, tourist buses were disgorging busy little bunches of the faithful, priests of every nationality, nuns clucking with their broods of children, Africans, Chinese, Indians, and of course, the ever-present sellers of 'gold plated' souvenirs. At 12 o'clock a banner was thrown over the distant windowsill, and the tiny figure appeared. Cameras whirred and the Pope boomed out over loudspeakers his message of peace to the world.

One evening we went to the Son et Lumiere pageant in the Roman Forum. We heard Mark Antony's speech spoken in the spot near to where Caesar was assassinated, horses' hooves and the shouting of crowds where armies returned victorious down the Sacred Way. We saw the temple of the Vestal Virgins glowing red with flames as the story of the fire in the Emperor Nero's time was told. There were some very convincing stereophonic lions roaring when the time came for the Christians to be eaten, and the Colosseum glowed with light a hundred yards away. As the tourist brochures would say, "This was the Rome experience."

On yet another evening we walked to the Borghese gardens as the evening light faded. We sat talking on a bench in

73

a small arbour overlooking the winding paths. He told stories about his studies at the university of Louvain in Belgium, a centre of advanced theological thinking. He and his best friend Cyril had been sent there and found on arrival that the lectures were held in French. They were expected to learn the language on their feet. As he said:

"Sometimes I knew they were talking about murder but I wasn't sure whether they were for it or agin' it!" In comparison the oral examinations in Latin seemed easy!

He spoke with feeling about the continued years of getting up at 5.15 for two hours of hungry prayers before breakfasts of hearty Belgian bread with cheese or chocolate spread. Despite this, the hungry young seminarians salivated when they smelled frites being cooked outside the railway station. They could never afford to buy any. Hearing about the young clerics with their tonsures and black robes wading through the puddles and endless rain of Belgium on their way to lectures I was impressed by the discipline of the life he and his fellow students had led. I would never have been able to resist the frites. There were weekend art excursions to other Belgian cities and to the mountains but study was always on his mind. Lighter moments came with a family living next door to the seminary who adopted him. He spent happy times with the children as a 'big brother'. The family became an important human balance to to the disciplined life of monastic prayer and study. He played with the five young girls, and they teased him and corrected his french. Their mother, an academic, treated him as the son she had never had. At the end of four years he graduated with a Magna Cum Laude. Despite persuasion to continue to a doctorate he was desperate to begin work and was thrilled to be posted to Zululand (now KwaZulu Natal). He left for Africa just one month after ordination in 1961. With sadness in his eyes he told me that when he had said farewell he knew that his father was suffering from a heart condition.

It was known, though unspoken, that they would not meet again. His father gave him a gold cross made from his Mother's wedding ring.

Slowly the light in the Borghese gardens faded as we talked. The numbers of walkers in the gardens had dwindled when we finally looked at our watches. It was midnight. We suddenly realised that this was 22nd September, the day the clocks were due to go back for Autumn. We had been unexpectedly gifted with another hour together. It was as though we were in a time slip and had been given a magical present!

However there were other matters on our minds. The church chosen for my longed-for reception into the Catholic Church was San Silvestro, an imposing pillared building reputed to contain the head of John the Baptist. That may or may not have been so, but the main reason for the choice seemed to be that it was the "English Church" in Rome and so seemed appropriate to Kieran and his confrères who were organising the ceremony. The arrangements were made. Kieran's word was taken that I was well prepared and we spent time planning the readings for the occasion. We chose Psalm 139

"Though I take the wings of the morning, and dwell in the uttermost parts of the sea, Still you shall lead me and your right hand upholds me." – a mutual favourite.

As we had indeed both flown from the uttermost parts of the sea it seemed a good choice. We could not know then that it would play an ongoing part in our lives.

Kieran's suggestion for a reading was from Luke's gospel describing the annunciation of Jesus' coming to Mary. He was in awe of this very young girl's simplicity of acceptance and I sensed in him an immense desire to achieve that same state. We made a trip to a bookshop in the Galleria in the Corso to buy a copy of "Prayers of Life" by Michel Quoist.

I was introduced to a poem called "Help me to say yes", which began:

"I am afraid of saying 'Yes', Lord. Where will you take me? I am afraid of drawing the longer straw, I am afraid of signing my name to an unread agreement, I am afraid of the 'yes' that entails other 'yeses'."

I was perfectly happy to read the poem. At the time I was not aware of being afraid at all, just happy to take this step. A very small and gentle English Servite priest who was coming to the ceremony sidled up to me and asked gently

"Are you very afraid? I know I should be." I was rather puzzled by his attitude. I was treading on a cushioned mat of faith, happiness and confidence. In retrospect I should have taken him very seriously indeed.

A few days before the reception ceremony an old acquaintance called Freddie arrived in Rome. Freddie was a ship's engineer I had met on a cruise around Australia with my parents some years before. He had worn a dashing uniform in those days and we had stayed in tenuous contact. He thought he had a closer relationship with me than he did. In any case, he was in Rome and we met by the Spanish Steps. Freddie was in the throes of a divorce, grieving the loss of parents and in a state of extreme negativity about the world. He was wearing a brown checked suit and heavy brogues which looked odd in summertime Rome, hated Italian food and constantly described himself as "Bitter and twisted" as though that was something to be admired. In the time since we had met he seemed to have become a fanatical Freemason with an abiding hatred of the Catholic Church. Rome, with a young woman about to become a member of this church was not the ideal place for him and it was even worse when he learned of my friendship with Father Kieran. We met up and walked around Rome, as he ranted in a state of near breakdown. It was a torment for both of us. Perhaps he had seen me as some kind of port in a storm. There was nothing I could do to calm him and eventually he left. But if I had been inclined to believe the medieval stories of demonic attack in order to swerve human souls from a spiritual purpose, I would imagine that the onslaught of such negative energies might have felt very similar. Those nights of attack were exhausting. The next day Kieran called at the hotel for the preliminary 'confession" or reconciliation – a spiritual clearing of the decks before dedication to a new beginning. I was almost too tired to remember what he had come for. We sat on the steps by the Ponte Sant'Angelo and shared again very simply the personal regrets and revelations we had already confided to each other.

The day dawned. It was office work as usual and grappling with the golfball typewriter. In the early evening I presented myself at the church of San Marcello and we walked across to San Silvestro. I chose to wear a bright green dress rather than an alternative grey one because it seemed such a joyous occasion. I was accompanied by Kieran, his friend Father Neil, (who was no fool and had raised one quizzical eyebrow about our relationship), Father Corr, the gentle English priest, and Father Joe Loftus, the American Father General of the Order.

San Silvestro was open and illuminated when we arrived. The gilded round arches shone in the light of the massive chandeliers and the high altar glittered in gilt and marble. Over the altar was a copy of the Mandylion, – a serious faced icon of Christ. Standing there at the altar, surrounded by priests, in the brilliantly lit space, I felt lifted, as though we were looking down on the scene from above, taking part in something momentous, the continuation in time of a mystical tradition of ceremonies that might have preceded this one through the ages. There was no need to be baptised, – that had been done when I was a baby but I renewed the promises made then on my behalf. We did the readings thoughtfully and I was welcomed into the church and thoroughly blessed. It had been a long wait since childhood to 'belong'.

When it was over and the paper records had been signed, I looked around, expecting to feel different. In the far right hand corner of the church, stood a woman. She seemed to have been present throughout. I was feeling elated so while the priests were tidying up, I ran down the church full of happiness intending to thank her for being there. She was a woman with features so perfect that one can fail to notice their beauty. She had brown hair and was wearing very unremarkable, even dowdy clothes in shades of brown. I addressed her in Italian, then in French, then in English. She just stood, smiling and serene without replying. I presumed she didn't speak any of those languages so just smiled at her and turned to go. When I next turned round she had disappeared. Who was she? Had we been entertaining an angel unawares?

After the ceremony we returned to the monastery at San Marcello and went upstairs into the refectory where there was a small roof garden. American Father Neil had cooked his special hamburgers and Father Joe had made a jug of stupendous martini, which was very strong indeed. If I had been feeling elated before the elation increased tenfold. Kieran was afraid I might cast caution to the winds and fling my arms around him. No such indiscretion occurred but navigating our way back to the Albergo del Sole the piazzas seemed to be shimmering and the fountains dancing. Everything had definitely moved several streets to the left or right that night.

The Curia work was coming to an end. Father Corr, the small, gentle English priest took me aside and asked if I would consider representing him at an International Ecumenical Conference discussing the unity of Christian churches, in a place called Gwatt, in Switzerland. I was not sure what this would entail but it sounded like another adventure. I was told firmly that I should meet up with two women, Lady Astor and Flora Glendon Hill. I was very doubtful about this. They sounded like upper-crust Englishwomen who would do good and wear funny hats.

When I went to the Monastery Bursar to be paid for the two weeks' office work I was shocked to be given a substantial amount, more than I had expected, which would exactly cover the fares and cost of the conference. Father Corr swore he had nothing to do with it. I had heard of this kind of thing happening, usually to evangelical missionaries down to their last crust but had never experienced it before.

It was time to return to Perugia. I packed up at the dusty Albergo del Sole. Kieran was preparing to go to Spain for the important General Chapter. We met at the bus terminal outside the Baths of Diocletian in the fading autumn sunshine. The air was tinged with chill. So were our emotions. We knew it was finally goodbye. We had no way of knowing whether we would ever meet again. It seemed very unlikely. We ran out of words. There was so much we had said, so much we could say but somehow speech seemed to have lost its power and meaning leaving only pain in the silence. We exchanged an awkward semi-hug and for the first and only time, we kissed. We were both crying. Kieran turned abruptly on his heel and walked away to hide his tears.

The bus journey back to Perugia seemed very long.

6
ECUMENICAL ADVENTURES.

A week or so later, at the end of September, I set out with a ticket to the International Ecumenical Conference in Gwatt in my pocket not knowing much about how to get there. However divine providence seemed to come along with the ticket. A group of loquacious Swiss Italians frogmarched me onto the right part of the train when it was about to split in half at Thun on the Swiss border. We arrived at Gwatt on a dark, rainy night. Another guardian angel appeared in the form of an elderly German gentleman, charming and fussy, who materialised out of the mist apparently with the sole purpose of giving directions. I was placed on a bus in a thick fog, put in charge of the driver and delivered like a parcel to the conference centre. Everything seemed to flow, in contrast to the usual reversals of travel. Shown to a pretty and comfortable room with blue curtains, I fell asleep. When I pulled the curtains in the morning the Alps were outside the window, icy and massive.

The conference was like living in a strange dream. It was a religious potpourri. There were delegates from archbishops to accountants and they represented more countries than I could have imagined and more branches of Christianity than I knew existed. I had no idea that people got together in this way and at this time in the late 1960s it was rare. One could be breakfasting with an Archimandrite or an Anchorite, or with a prim Methodist lady from Haywards Heath. And even she was likely to have hidden degrees or titles. There were lectures in English, French, German, and Spanish, discussions, and daily liturgies to experience from all of the varieties of faith represented. I was far too fascinated and busy to go in search of the two ladies I was supposed to meet. When glimpsed they did not wear funny hats. Lady Astor was tall, patrician and beautiful which was not surprising as I learned later that she had been a fashion model of some renown in Paris. Flora Glendon Hill, the President of the organisation was small, plump and cuddly. She had dimples and seemed to laugh a lot. She was rarely still and flitted around the conference leaving a trail of files, papers, handbags and cigarette lighters behind her. Listening to her charismatic final address it seemed to me that she was like a St Teresa of Avila character with a dash of technicolour thrown in. It was only on the last night after the candlelight closing that I realised I should do something to meet her and trailed around with her abandoned handbag to return it and introduce myself. Finally I tracked her down in her room and knocked at the door. She was sitting up in bed wearing a pink nightdress.

"I've come to return your handbag," I said. She patted the bed next to her to sit down. I was just about to explain that I had been sent by Father Gerry Corr in Rome when she said:-

"So you're another one!"

"Another what?" I said.

"Another fool for the sake of Christ!" was the reply.

This threw me. Who was this person who quoted St Paul at midnight wearing a pink frilly nightdress?

There was not much time to talk. The conference was ending. It was arranged that I should accompany her and a busload of Americans to Lausanne and meet up in Geneva. This I did. Travelling with the Americans was diverting. They were astonished at everything. When the bus stopped briefly in Lausanne the cathedral was being restored and was shrouded in scaffolding. The elderly lady in the next

seat had fallen asleep. She woke up just in time to hear that
it had been built in the 13th Century. She sat up with a start
and said:

"My God and they haven't finished it yet!"

Flora, wearing her best black coat had gone ahead to
Geneva, with a hectic timetable of visits to church councils
and dignitaries. By the time we arrived at the hotel it was
overbooked so we had to share a room.

I thought we would sleep, But this was Flora.

I do not know exactly what happened that night. Flora
was a highly experienced psychologist and counsellor and I
found myself telling her all the events of the past few
months and much besides. Conversation dwelt on the relationship with Kieran and all the inner joy, conflict and pain
it had caused. Late in the night I found myself almost physically forced by an unknown power to kneel down and say
"yes" to whatever suffering might be ahead. The possibilit-
ies seemed to include the essence of all the many crucifixion
scenes I had seen above church altars and in particular the
humiliation and abasement of such a fate. The terrible de-
gradation was completely vivid and real. I had no idea what
it meant. In the course of the night too, towards morning I
had a most vivid dream in which Kieran and I were walking
hand in hand, as tall naked souls among a landscape which
consisted of enormous pillars stretching endlessly upwards
until they disappeared in a thick mist. It was only some time
later that I realised that trees and towers do in fact disappear
upwards in thick fog. In Australia I had never seen those
weather conditions.

The next day, feeling shattered, we had bread and soup
in a mist-shrouded cafe overlooking Lake Geneva. At the
beginning of the meal Flora took a bread roll, broke it and
shared it. I began to ask some questions about spirituality
and prayer. She seemed like the sort of person who might

have some answers. It was a relief to find that it might not be necessary to say ten minutes of words every morning and night. It began to seem as if deep prayer – meditation – contemplation might be more a matter of silence, and of going deep inside oneself – I saw it as an endless cone spiralling into the dark inside my mind.

We parted with invitations for Christmas in England with Flora and her work partner Mary Tanner. After some horse-trading with rail tickets I took the train back to Perugia, fortified with a few bars of Swiss chocolate- comfort eating always being a refuge in times of stress. Listening to the clack clack clack of the train I realised that all the happiness of the Italian summer had been wiped out. The joy was completely gone. In its place was a world where the sunlight had turned to hard iron grey and there was a burning spot in the centre of my forehead, like the proverbial coal of fire. An obnoxious young man made a pass at me and tried for a kiss and I simply walked through him as though he was a bothersome insect or a feather. The world seemed to have become irrelevant to me and I had become an irrelevance in the world. Nothing mattered. But at the same time, in some inexplicable way, everything had undergone a permanent change and I had crossed a bridge from belief to knowledge. From then on the concept of mere 'belief 'would always seem weak and colourless. As a friend would say in the future – "If a man were to say to his wife, "I believe I love you, what would she think?"

Back in Perugia the summer had come to an end. The weather had broken, the rain had come and the steep streets were running with water. The outdoor cafe tables were piled up and abandoned and the University was further emptying out as summer students returned home. The last weeks of lectures seemed drained of meaning. The advanced courses, the drama and music, the commercial Italian that had seemed so promising all passed by unnoticed. I sat in a class and wrote a poem about an apple orchard in the rain, not realising how prophetic it would be.

It was time to pack up and embark on the next part of the trip, two weeks in each of Florence and Rome. Having been bidden farewell by Signora Mercouri Ridolfi with a breakfast of 'Zuppa Inglese' (English soup?) which closely resembled trifle, we set off for the beauties of Renaissance Florence.

It was a terrible dark grey time. Summer had gone. Autumn had come and the city was full of fallen leaves, black skies and rain. I walked around the Uffizi with blind eyes. Neither Michelangelo nor Botticelli seemed to have any meaning. To my astonishment I began to wake up in the Pensione Anna in the small hours with unexpected and involuntary tears streaming down my face. Getting up quietly I would dress and desperately walk the streets, at two or three in the morning, oblivious to the hooting and laughter of passing young blades in their sports cars.

Rome was no better. There were autumn leaves blowing along by the Tiber as our feet crackled through them. I was blind to the glories of past empires and the beauties of the Vatican Museum. We visited the Sistine Chapel, and the masculine breasted nudes of Michelangelo's tomb. The wind howled through the streets and seemed to howl through life itself. Even the Italian shoe shops had lost their allure. Finally I gave up and realised it was useless to stay any longer. The light had gone out of life. Persuaded by wise Mme Ladomirska I bought a ticket and set off for England, via Paris to spend Christmas with Flora and her business partner Mary about whom I knew little. I travelled without much hope.

After a short stay in Paris, I boarded the ferry for Dover. It was my first encounter with British culture. As I went up the gangway I tripped slightly and was righted by a jolly sailor with an "Oops Love!" This was new – were all English people comedians? Having ordered a coffee – or was it tea? – at the cafeteria, I tasted the pale grey liquid and couldn't decide.

By making enquiries I found that to reach my destination in Sussex I would need to take a train north to Victoria station and then a second train back in a south easterly direction. As I would discover this was standard procedure when travelling on British trains since all the lines radiate from London with no cobweb tracks in between. In contrast to the vivacity of Italian travellers, British people with dead-pan faces sat facing each other in carriages, giving no sign that they recognised their neighbours as human beings. If possible they hid behind newspapers. They might have been rows of shop mannequins. The trains were hermetically sealed, hot and musty and the seats were upholstered in prickly blue checked velvet. At Victoria station I was surprised by the level of litter on the concourse, – people were wading ankle deep in blowing waste paper. A train arrived and I was astonished to see dark suited gentlemen alighting with briefcases, bowler hats and umbrellas like a scene from a comedy. I arrived in Three Bridges and found a taxi. The house, called Barnwood seemed difficult to find. The cockney taxi driver went up one dark lane after another, at one point saying "Cor, it's the ruddy crematorium now!"

Finally we arrived. A tall woman with dark hair and deep-set dark eyes opened the door, holding back a barking black cocker spaniel. This must be the mysterious Mary.

"Come in" she said. "Where have you been?" And practically, "You're all wet! Get those shoes off!"

Flora was called, I was picked up dried off and given a bowl of soup. There seemed to be a rather large number of boys in the background. I had arrived in the land of carpet slippers and common sense. I was shown into a cosy room with a green carpet and fell into bed.

The next morning, I began to find out more about the house where I had landed. The first surprise was the number of boys who were being given breakfast and ushered off to school. What was this place? Barnwood was a large house in West Sussex which had been acquired by three women some years before. Flora, a social worker, Mary a nurse, and Jean a teacher were friends, – Jean had died some years before- who had been struck by the number of so-called "latch-key kids" on the streets of London, vulnerable young people whose parents were working or absent and who came home from school with nothing to do. Predictably many of them found themselves in difficult situations and developed mental or behavioural problems. The three women applied to run a Therapeutic Unit in the country, a kind of foster home, where a number of boys could live and be cared for while they went to school and received appropriate therapy from visiting psychologists. The boys had a safe comfortable home with a large games room, all they could eat, three qualified "aunties", supervision and sensible amounts of freedom. What they did not realise was that in these women with their varied training and talents they had foster parents who passionately cared about them and whose lives ran on integrity and prayer. The small community relied on mutual care and trust. In contrast to some of the High Schools where I had taught, there was an atmosphere of extraordinary peace and harmony. The young people helped and supported each other, and co-operated with the order and watchfulness exercised very subtly by the "Aunties". Some of the boys had histories of arson, theft, and mayhem but the home was a model of mutual support. When the occasional row or tantrum broke out, there was a united front to solve the problem. The daily details of the house were seen to by Dora, a sharp-tongued local woman with bright yellow hair, and loud, cockney Peggy, who cooked copious amounts of filling and stodgy food for young appetites.

It was early December. The days were cold but the house was cosy. Conversations with Flora continued interspersed with preparations for Christmas. The boys would go home, Mary would travel to a relative and I had the chance to go with Flora for Christmas at York Minster where her nephew was among the clergy.

I had begun to realise that this was a very unusual house. To begin with, the two women at the helm seemed to live their faith in an extraordinarily wholehearted way. While both practical people, capable of dealing with crises efficiently, and possessed of a quick and raucous sense of humour, both were women of deep prayer and daily churchgoing and times of prayer were natural parts of their day. Life with Flora meant being challenged mentally and psychologically. Topics which began on the surface could end up plumbing psychological depths. And our relationship quickly developed into one that was that of teacher and pupil, spiritual guide and aspirant, therapist and young woman in search of wholeness. Flora was a scholar as well as a mystic and a leader. I was introduced to the concept of the Mantra, ancient writings on prayer and works by scholars from Orthodox and Eastern traditions.

I also began to observe the relationship of the two women. Both were individualists, who led their own lives, and both had very different personalities and practical roles in the house. They were friends and working partners, not in any way a sexual couple. But when Flora spoke of Mary it was with a sense of reverence, as though she was 'special' in some way. I hadn't yet seen that, and yet her tall middle-aged beauty and penetrating, deep set dark eyes hinted at a depth that I had not so far met in any of my acquaintances.

PAMELA O'CUNEEN

One night, feeling nervous and depressed, I left my room and went prowling to the kitchen for a snack, prey to an outbreak of comfort eating. As I walked along the dark passage to the kitchen I had a strange feeling that Mary knew perfectly well what I was doing although she was, as far as I knew, sound asleep in her bedroom. It was not a comfortable feeling.

Early in December a letter came from Kieran saying that the General Chapter and Conference was over and he was at a clinic in Paris, receiving treatment for his back which had gone into painful spasm, probably caused by sleeping on sagging dormitory beds in the conference centre. Could I come over to France? Incredulous with joy at this unexpected reunion, I booked a ferry passage and took myself to Paris. We met up in the cold, damp December weather, looking unfamiliarly muffled up in coats and hats. Paris was dark and unlit. It felt that we were walking around in a bleak underworld. We only had a few days, just time to look at Notre Dame, to have a meal or two together and time for some freezing walks by the Seine, curtailed by Kieran's back problems. We got no further in discussions, and we were both less than our normal selves. But I learned that he had spoken out at the Chapter in Spain about the outdated ideas he had encountered regarding "missionary activities" and had expressed some revolutionary theories as to what he felt should be the role of modern missionaries – which was to uplift people while respecting the local culture. He asserted that it should not be about making head counts of baptised souls. He was promptly and unanimously given the task, to tour the world for a year, visit all Servite missions, write assessments of them and then return and report to the various General Chapters around Europe and America. Since the missions existed in Africa, India and around Latin America this was a major undertaking. A lesser man might have wished he had kept his mouth shut but Kieran was excited

88

at the prospect. He just needed to regain his strength before departing in the New Year. He would spend Christmas in Ireland and then leave on his round the world travels. There was a slight ray of hope for us too. It seemed as though he might need to take his first flight via London. Perhaps, just perhaps we might meet again before he left. I went back to England and Barnwood, feeling a little more hopeful. And there was Christmas to look forward to.

Flora and I travelled by car from Sussex to York for Christmas. It was a long journey and my first experience of motorway driving in the dark slush and rain. We stopped on the way in English pubs for meals and I was astonished and appalled by the dark red and puce decor, with red lamps and hectically patterned floral and swirled carpets. There were many new things to experience. We were constantly seeing something called "Flyovers" but nothing seemed to be flying, there were things called 'lay byes" – which in Australia meant a scheme to put aside an item in a shop and pay for it in instalments. Here in England they seemed to be parking places by the side of the road. But I was impressed with how optimistic and positive people in England seemed to be, since every few miles we passed a quaint looking building with big signs saying "Courage!" It was many months before I realised that this was the name of a brand of beer and that the buildings were in fact pubs.

York's medieval streets were as brightly lit with Christmas lights and full of bustling cheerful people. We arrived on Christmas Eve and were welcomed to the "Precentors House" overlooking the towers of York Minster itself. The family was all that I could have hoped an English clerical family might be, with two little girls wildly excited about Christmas. On Christmas Eve it began to snow. I had only seen snow on Christmas cards printed in Australia, where it was always represented by white blobs about the size of cricket balls. It seemed as though it might be quite dangerous to be hit by one of these blobs. But looking out into the night, this stuff that they said was snow was coming down like a shower of fine icing sugar. How could it ever coat a landscape? The next morning I found out. There was a white carpet outside the windows. Christmas morning service in the enormous York Minster, the ceremony of the life-sized crib and traditional Christmas dinner were all that could be wished for. Wearing the warmest coat I had and a newly acquired furry hat I went for a walk and was urged by Flora to walk on some snow for a photograph. It proved to be a snowdrift as she well knew. There was the chance to be taken up into the roof of York Minster in the cradle being used by restorers and to gaze at golden angels face to face. Driving round the countryside in the snow I was asked to map-read, and used as I was to Australian country distances, I was astonished by the rapidity with which the small villages followed each other. Most of the time we were through the next village before I had read its name.

Back in Barnwood there was a letter from Kieran saying that he would come through England in January and would arrange to come to Gatwick airport, only five miles away.

On the day he was due I was loaned the car and drove, hugely daring, to meet him. Gatwick was a very small airport in those days with only one terminal, and I proudly negotiated the concrete not- very- multi level parking building. There he was, rugged up, wearing a Russian style hat, looking both tentative and shiny with happiness. We drove safely back to Barnwood to warmth, tea and scones by the fire. Flora and Mary seemed to find Kieran as easy to talk to as I did and the evening was long, with stories about Africa. Their listening skills drew out his childhood history of the loss of his Mother, the unkind and sadistic childrens' homes, and his distress at being sidelined in Zululand. He told us about his love for his Zulu friends, their singing and dancing together and all night Easter vigils. We learned that he had even been poisoned, or perhaps bewitched for a stance he had taken. It was as though he was at home and able to open his heart in the company of people who would understand.

At bedtime we had a brief insight into who Mary really was. Kieran mentioned that since the conference in Spain all the skin on his fingertips was red, sore and peeling due to stress.. Nothing seemed to help. "Let me see," said Mary. We presumed she was using her professional nurse's eye. But she held his two hands in hers, and closed her eyes for a moment. A deep silence descended on the room. "That should be better now, "she said. The next morning the skin was healed.

The next day was freezing cold but we took Flora's car and drove to the nearest town, Brighton, where we tried to enjoy the cold grey sea, and had tea and some uninspiring stale scones. We were enjoying each other's company far more. When we were together we were enclosed not only in the car but in a bubble of happiness, all the more precious because of its fragility and the knowledge that it was likely to be punctured and blown away sooner rather than later.

When we arrived back at Barnwood I lost Kieran for a while. He was tracked down in the boys' games room, with the youngsters gathered around him, playing an energetic game of table tennis. Flora suggested that we might arrange a house Mass. On the following day, his last, it was set up. The boys in the house went to church on Sundays with a fairly good grace but like most young boys, it was on sufferance. This, however was different. Kieran's charisma fired their enthusiasm. They were invited to 'preach the sermon' by saying what they thought the readings meant, there was singing of modern songs and dancing. Suddenly church had become fun. "When's Father Kieran going to do another house Mass Auntie?" was the constant question.

On the same evening I crept up to his little attic room. It was cold under the roof. Not having encountered a blow heater before Kieran had put it into his bed to warm it up causing a mini explosion and a horrible smell of cordite. Having rescued the heater I sat on the bed beside him, since there was no chair, and we talked about the future that could never be. He told me how much he loved the children in Zululand, and choked up when he thought of children we might have had together if things were different. Just for a few moments we allowed ourselves to fantasise about them – a boy called Kieran Francis and a girl called Chiara.

The next evening we were all talking quietly in Mary's room when the atmosphere in the room became silent and intense. Mary closed her eyes and began to speak very slowly in a low sweet voice, nothing like her normal voice which could be strong and at times even quite raucous. Flora grabbed a pen and paper. We realised this was something that had happened before, many times. Mary was addressing words to Kieran, but in phrases that were completely different from her usual speech patterns.

Kieran was addressed as "Beloved son of my heart". He was told that the pattern of his life would "change and change again because I desire that you should be one of those who have been chosen to help fulfil my divine will in this world." … "Have great faith in my love. I am forever with you, guarding and guiding all your days for indeed I have great need of you. Unto you I give many many souls."

"It is for you to take My heart out into the desert places of this world and to draw together into that heart all those whom you meet by the wayside, on the mountains and in the valleys, in the high places and in the plain. Gather them in, secure within my heart. This is for you and for all who know me as only those who love can know. My beloved priest, fear not for the morrow. Fear not for anything. All my love is within you and without you and around you forever and forever."

By the time this message had been given Kieran's brown eyes were as round as saucers. Was this a message from God? He was speechless. Mary and Flora on the other hand, while reverent, were unfazed and Mary in particular said something like "Well that's that then". Flora promised to type out the message for him by morning. After a cup of tea we all departed to bed with a lot to think about.

In the small hours of the next morning Kieran came downstairs to my room, shivering and cold after a disturbing dream. He had woken up with the imperative in his mind to "find Pamela". Without a second thought I peeled back the blankets and he crawled in to warm up. We lay there, just holding each other as close as possible, clutched desperately as though we were on a life raft in danger of being swept over Niagara Falls. It was all we had. All we could do.

7

THE DEPARTURE

It was January 1969 and Kieran's last morning before he left for the year's travelling. He wanted to say Mass before he went. It was just Kieran, Flora, Mary and me. We set up a little table in my room. The atmosphere was charged with the imminent departure. All the readings seemed to have great import. Just before the consecration Flora took off a ring she wore and gave it to Kieran saying, –

"Give this to Pamela." She had no idea why she did this and had no prior intention of doing so.

Immediately he put it on the silver plate with the communion host, blessed it and placed it on the third finger of my left hand. The atmosphere was electric. We were both surprised and shocked at this unexpected action – it had not been planned or intended. It seemed portentous, outrageous even. What could it mean? What did it imply? At the end of the Mass, overcome by emotion, Kieran's legs gave way and he collapsed to the floor.

I have no memory of the farewell or of who took him to the airport. Probably it was Flora. After he went I lay on the floor for some time, feeling pain in every cell, my skin so sensitive I could not bear to be touched, unable even to cry. For several days I seemed to have a second heartbeat, – probably due to stress – but it was tempting to think that our hearts had joined in some mysterious way. I wondered if Kieran too, was experiencing a second heartbeat.

He sent a note soon afterwards saying that he felt that he would be completely safe on this trip and that all would go well, since we had something important to do together in the future.

It took some time to process these events. They felt momentous but I had no idea what they meant for the present or the future. Was this a spiritual marriage? I imagined that we were meant to live with a deep spiritual bond, that I was destined to be a kind of Clare to his Francis, supporting his work. Meantime life at Barnwood continued as usual, helping with the house administration, typing letters for Flora's ecumenical work and editing an article Flora was writing on the English Mystics. I had asked if I could stay for a while, as it felt comfortable and it seemed that I could be useful in the house. It was a time of deep spirituality. There was an experience after which I no longer had any fear of death, and knew beyond any doubt that the spiritual dimension was more vivid, and more real than anything we could experience in the material world.

Easter came and I was awed at the seriousness with which Good Friday was commemorated in the house. There was an atmosphere of solemnity. Mary spent most of the day in her room praying and meditating. On Holy Saturday we all went into the garden gathering daffodil buds and cutting a lot of seemingly bare branches. The flowers and branches were brought into the warm house and placed in water. By the following day the daffodils had opened and the bare branches had sprouted buds and were forming fresh tender green leaves. I had never witnessed this before. It was a real celebration of new life. And Easter eggs had their place too – far more appreciated by the boys.

One night in early May, quite late, at about ten to eleven, the three of us were talking quietly when once again that immense hush descended on the room, as though someone had turned down the volume to zero.

Mary's eyes closed once more and she began speaking in the lower, sweeter voice that I was beginning to recognise. She spoke slowly, in a measured way, using poetic phrases that she would never normally use. Once more she did not seem to be speaking as herself. Among her words were these, spoken slowly and taken down carefully by Flora.

"I have given unto you a vocation which means many, many trials. Indeed there will be set before you a period of training which will give you all those graces necessary for the fulfilment of your vocation.

"Remember always my own beloved priest. He is beloved by so many and most dearly by you. Unite yourself completely in this love for indeed I have given this love and made it one – his for you and yours for him and mine for you both but great love always overcomes and is strengthened by its many trials. Your futures and the future of many will depend upon your love, one for another, in purity and holiness.

"It is for you and those who are like you, to loosen the bonds and free the love, to unite together that all men may be free – free to Love and free to be loved and free to find within that love the expression of God's mind for the world. Ask and pray. Ask and it shall be given unto you in wisdom and in a knowledge of my truth.

"Pray for all men who would love that they may find the purity and the beauty that is within their own hearts. Pray this, my child and rejoice and be glad, for unto you has been given a treasure beyond price and into your safe-keeping has been given a treasure from my own heart."

The words continued:

"Be faithful be kind, have pity upon all those who would love, but fear love and all shall be well and indeed all manner of thing shall be well, and there shall be a new earth and a new people and a new way for each man to walk.

"Give my love unto the one you love and the one I love and ask him when he offers the cup of my love, to think of the great love which I have poured down for him and for you and for all men, and in the thinking to gather up the souls within his heart and taking them every one, to fill and refill that cup which he holds, that I may give back a hundredfold all that is given and offered unto me.

"Give him my blessing even as I bless you this night and for ever more."

The message ended at ten past eleven. A lot for a mere human being to compose so perfectly and fluently in such a short time, particularly someone like Mary who was an eminently practical person and not particularly highly educated.

It was a lot to take in. In fact I did not take it in and didn't fully realise that the message was directed to me – initially it seemed that it was not – and for some reason I felt completely bereft and cried inconsolably for a long time after it ended. Exhausted with grief, I finally realised that the message was a recognition of our love for each other. But it was hard to see what it could mean for the future. It felt of great importance, but how it could work out in reality was a mystery. I read and re-read the words, wondering.

(These inspired messages from Mary were a phenomenon known then in theological circles as 'locutions'. Since such things were regarded with great suspicion by the Church, Mary and Flora kept the events under wraps. Today, with spirituality of all kinds more widely known, similar occurrences are known as 'channelling' and are not regarded as particularly unusual.)

Meantime the year was progressing. A visit from my parents in Australia was due. We had not met for more than a year and I was due to meet them in London. I was only partially looking forward to the reunion since I felt I had become a very different person in the intervening year, and that, parent-like they would expect their daughter to be the same. And there had been deep changes. In particular I had explored my relationship with Mother in depth and expected to react differently to her.

What I had not bargained for was that my strong, feisty Mother was feeling quite dwarfed by this new world in which she found herself. She had been a strong woman all her life, first in the country in North-Western Australia and then in the small city of Perth. London was a different matter. Very big, very strange and very busy. I realised how she was feeling when we crossed a busy road and her hand clutched mine like a frightened little claw. Dad, on the other hand was his calm phlegmatic self with the dry Australian sense of humour I loved. They were invited down to Barnwood for a few days and I met them at the station. I am not sure that Mother liked Flora and Mary very much, despite their best efforts at charm and hospitality. I suspect the whole setup with the boys and the busy household seemed very strange to her and she may have thought that Mary and Flora were in a lesbian relationship, if indeed she quite knew what that was. The parents went on their long-awaited tour of a lifetime round Europe and I received excited letters and postcards as they progressed. They were thrilled with everything they saw, although Mother was not impressed to see "so many old buildings" and found the lavatory arrangements very trying at times. Finally in late summer they returned. After their tour of the British Isles we decided to embark on a train journey together, visiting some countries they had not seen. We set off together, booking accommodation as we went, and visiting Paris, Munich – where we visited Dachau together, and Vienna which seemed far too overwhelming and grand to take in. On the way back we stayed in Zurich where they had their first fondue. It was strange to be the leader and guide, having previously been subservient and junior in the family. I remember sitting for long hours as the trains glided through Europe, my mind filled with endless longing thoughts of Kieran, but talking about everything else, since I had no intention of mentioning him. Tell Mother that I was in love with a Catholic priest? She who believed religion should be taken with a pinch of salt? Certainly not!

It was only at the very end of the trip, when I was on a train alone with my father, that he broached the subject saying

"Who is this Kieran chap?"

Apparently a whisper had travelled all the way to Australia. I managed, I hoped, to convince him that Kieran was just a friend who didn't matter very much.

After the summer it seemed that my time in Barnwood was coming to an end. I began looking for teaching posts and found one as a teacher of English as a Foreign language in Eastbourne, a very traditional British seaside town about forty miles away. I was interviewed in a small Stately Home by the grim and redoubtable headmistress and got the job. There was a small flat available in the town and one hot day, wearing my most efficient navy blue and white dress, I went by train to see that as well. The flat consisted of a tiny kitchen and an unheated bedroom furnished with a bed and a brown leather sofa. The landlady, Rosemary, was sturdy, smiling and friendly and chiefly astonished that I was travelling without an umbrella in an English summer. It seemed like a good omen that she was an enthusiastic amateur cellist.

The time in Eastbourne was an insight into other aspects of English life. It was a glimpse into the past, an Edwardian town with a seaside promenade, a bandstand and a winter garden and a seaside theatre where genteel comedies were played and tea was served on trays during the interval. It

was also known as the 'Suntrap of the south' and was inhabited largely by extremely elderly people, most of whom
seemed to be wheeled around in wheelchairs with small
dogs on their laps. Teashops and scones proliferated. The
windswept beach was covered with stones which shocked
my Australian soul to the core. Where was the white sand?
The school, in Devonshire Place, a summer home of the
Duke of Devonshire, was a colonnaded mansion set in park-
land, full of crystal chandeliers and marble fireplaces. It was
the branch of a London language school where the richest
pupils were housed, the equivalent of debutantes from a
dozen countries. The headmistress, Mrs Eva Engholm, was
a fierce woman in late middle age who dragged her hair into
a severe bun, wore T bar orthopaedic sandals and ruled the
establishment with a rod of iron. She was a keen bird lover
and liked to rescue oil covered penguins which she kept in
her flat in the bath. She also had a caged monkey in her
bedroom. Having written an English grammar book during
her time teaching in Kenya, she insisted that this should be
used in the school guaranteeing herself an ongoing income
The setting was luxurious, but the timetable and the discipline were severe. Meals were served in an ornate and over-
heated dining room and as one student remarked, "The
English eat five time a day and every time with custard". We
had students from a variety of countries – French girls who
hated the food, Chinese who worked extremely hard, South
Americans who didn't and liked to go to London in the
weekends to shop for jewellery and fur coats. There were
Arabic speakers who struggled with written work, and a
group of Italians who scandalised Mrs Engholm by taking
nude photographs of each other which they had developed
in the local Boots chemist and sold in the town. She seemed
chiefly annoyed by the fact that the photographs were developed in Boots. The plus side of the job was that every
weekend excursions were planned to beauty spots in the

south of England, and sometimes to London to increase the students' knowledge of English culture, which suited me well from a sightseeing point of view.

During the latter part of the time in Barnwood I had begun singing again and had auditioned for a famous singing teacher in London, Roy Henderson. I was drawn to him since he had taught one of my idols, Kathleen Ferrier. Prof Henderson was a small neat man who had been a renowned tenor in his day. He taught in a studio in Hampstead. He wore a velvet smoking jacket and a bow tie. His small white poodle sat on a couch and listened, her ears cocked, to the lessons. Prof was delightful, and had a habit of creeping up behind his sopranos and tickling them when he wanted a relaxed high note. I was fortunate to be accepted as a pupil. However, the next-door neighbour to the Eastbourne flat pounded with a broom on the wall whenever I practised, driving me to near despair. My dear landlady Rosemary secured the key to a nearby church hall for peaceful afternoon practising. It had a fearsome echo and a much used piano but it was a refuge. She was understanding, since in a similar situation in her youth she had been reduced to practising her cello in a bus shelter on the seafront.

Loving handwritten letters came from Kieran at regular intervals. They came from Zululand where he reunited with his beloved Zulu friends and, one suspected, was not altogether flavour of the month with the Monsignor with whom he had disagreed, returning as he now did with the full weight of the Roman Curia behind him. Fortunately he was travelling with a saintly senior Italian priest Father Andrea Cecchin, who was adept at pouring oil on troubled waters. He visited Swaziland and met the old King Sobhuza II who had 200 wives. In Chile he was delighted to find that the main street was called "Avenida Libertador General Bernard O'Higgins", and from Argentina he sent a photograph of the "Bar Pamela". In Brazil, he visited Sao Paulo, and

Rio, and Rio Branco, but his most cherished experiences were in Acre in the far south where he slept in hammocks and was flown in tiny single engined aircraft over the rain forest, which looked like fields of broccoli. The plane was shot at by startled Amerindians aiming their bows and arrows. It all seemed very exotic and far away but each letter was devoured and cherished.

During this year there was much talk in Barnwood about the import of some of Mary's messages. They seemed to imply that the two women and others who would join them should found a kind of centre for spiritual growth and healing. This would be commonplace now but in the late 1960s it was so unusual as to be almost unheard of. But everyone who heard of the idea seemed to be attracted to it. There was discussion of winding up the work with the boys, most of whom were reaching the end of their school days, and buying a property, particularly as Mary's health and eyesight were deteriorating.

In Eastbourne, during the winter term I was becoming increasingly subject to bouts of depression. Brief and rare at first, they increased rapidly so that on waking I would check to see if the black cloud was there and it was a wonderful morning it it was absent. It became an effort to keep going. Finally, after I had struggled for some time, I shared the problem with Flora and a good friend called Elsa, a vicar's wife and simultaneous translator for the Ecumenical movement. She recommended a man with a peculiar name who had helped her in the past. He lived in London. I took the name and address and made an appointment, with no idea what he might do, but was prepared to do breathing exercises, starve or stand on my head if that was what was needed. And so I went to Ravenscourt Park in West London and met Oscar Köllerstrom.

Mr Köllerstrom was a surprise. He was a tall, thin, elderly man, who wore a beard, a bow tie, a monocle and black and white spats. His appearance took me aback at first. I felt I had stepped into another century. He was very formal and lived in a house that was full of curios and sculptures and velvet settees. His consulting room had a huge desk, an arm-chair, and a long hard antique couch upholstered in blue velvet, with fierce carved dragons heads on the arms – I always felt that they might bite. It seemed that he was a psychoanalyst (I privately resolved to look up what that was exactly) and we were going to talk. I was motioned to lie on the couch and he sat slightly behind me in true Freudian style. And so began a journey of four years of self-exploration and discovery.

I would take the train to London once a week and travel to Ravenscourt Park never knowing what the session would involve. I began by talking about the present but the conversation soon switched to early childhood experiences and my feeling of alienation from my mother, who had admitted that, as an unexpected baby born in her early 40s, I had not exactly been welcome. Mother was not a warm or huggy person, and like many of her generation, felt that to praise children was tantamount to 'spoiling' them. In extreme situations she resorted to the old fashioned application of the back of a hairbrush which was effective, though more humiliating than painful. The feeling I had had of being some kind of changeling surfaced and I felt, obscurely that it was necessary to dredge up my most ignoble thoughts and actions. Mr K simply listened. Some of the most difficult revelations concerned the spiritual experiences with Mary and Flora. I felt that by revealing this period of life I might be regarded as certifiable. But Mr K just sat, and seemed to nod in approval when I said that had I come from another culture, the spiritual experiences would most likely have come in another form, featuring revelations of Shiva or the Buddha, perhaps. Once, I came with a beautifully written document about my feelings which was roundly rejected and ridiculed as being a false pose, – and it probably was. Mr K said very little, so that my words dropped into an ocean of listening silence slightly behind me and to the right. When I rebelled to the extent of querying the need to lie on the blue velvet couch, his reaction was to invite me to sit anywhere else I wanted, to sit on the floor if I preferred. I stayed on the couch. He had an uncanny knack of under-cutting any resistance to the process and leaving one stand-ing on the wrong foot. One day when I came in the depths of despair, threatening suicide he called my bluff and merely enquired in an interested voice

"What method are you considering – gas or electricity?" What could I do but laugh?

I was encouraged to remember and record dreams, and found, miraculously that by telling myself to remember them I could do so. By keeping a notepad by the bed they became available on waking, like a stream of bizarre, beau-tiful and frightening stories. I and learned to interpret them for myself. It became obvious that all dreams were meaning-ful, and that often the worst and most nightmarish night time experiences could be the most hopeful, since death and destruction could point unerringly to parts of the self that had been ignored or destroyed, or to an old phase of life, or a defence mechanism that was now ready to die. It had never occurred to me that it was possible to set out with the aim of conscious growth. I had assumed that people just felt the way they did and that everyone felt much the same. Groping week by week through a morass of feelings, and confessions, I gradually began to see that it was possible to understand oneself better, and in so doing to change one' s relationship with other people and with the world. The de-pression did not improve rapidly but slowly, and with the process of analysis, an intense desire to become a whole per-son set in. Freudian psychoanalysis is very unfashionable now, and regarded by many as a means of adjusting people to a neurotic world.

Oscar Köllerstrom was a wise man. He believed in handing over the task of analysis and dream interpretation to the analysand, and unshockable, took no prisoners when he spotted dishonesty or sentimentality. As the years went on, the visits to this magical and challenging world of analysis became a treasured part of life, a kind of inner adventure of discovery. I would not say that in analytical parlance, transference ever occurred to the extent of falling in love with my analyst, although I did feel a few twinges of mild jealousy when I spotted his beautiful ballerina wife drifting through the house in the distance.

There came a time when I was given permission to call him "Oscar" and he told me that he had trained with one of the original disciples of Freud, Georg Groddeck who was a pioneer of psychosomatic medicine, and that he had undertaken this training because as a priest of the Liberal Catholic Church he found he was unable to help people as he wished. He showed me a cross he wore, set with precious stones.

Oscar could be very disconcerting. One day I turned up having dyed my hair red and cut it very short. He opened the door and said, "Now why have you changed your persona?" On another day he was looking out of the window as I arrived for the appointment. He said, as I entered, "You looked like a flame as you walked through the square." I was not sure what to make of that but discovered much later that he had had the ability to see auras since childhood.

A result of beginning this period of psychoanalysis was the loss of my job in Eastbourne. I was stupid enough to ask for an afternoon off to go to London for the initial appointment and to admit to depression as the reason for going. The redoubtable Mrs Engstrom obviously decided she did not want a mentally unstable member of staff, and took the earliest opportunity to terminate my contract. I was initially taken aback by this brutality but the decision to move on at the end of the school year was now made.

Meantime property for the new Centre of Healing was being bought. Barnwood would be sold and with the financial help of Lady Astor a large house called Effingham Park was purchased in another part of Sussex, not far from Gatwick Airport, and the move was planned. It seemed an exciting prospect.

Effingham Park was an Edwardian house of dubious architectural merit with large gardens and acres of golden yellow drapes and carpet. Flora and Mary moved in with a few of the remaining senior boys. It was exciting but we felt rather dwarfed by the vastness of the property. In places it was even spooky. I would go through a glass conservatory to reach the piano and there was always a frisson as though I was being watched. One night one of the boys was tipped out of bed with his mattress on top of him. The other boys swore they had not played a trick – was there a poltergeist around?

Kieran was coming back for Christmas and this time he would spend it with us. He arrived as a member of the family. He was joyfully welcomed to Effingham Park as a loved returning son, with various small gifts collected on his travels, colourful scarves, beads and textiles from South America. We were grateful to Flora and Mary for giving us shelter and the chance to spend time together.

The winter was cold, snowy and sparkling, and there were few leaves on the trees apart from the remnants of some copper beech hedges. We went on long, cold walks, fearlessly hand in hand. It was a magical and protected time. Mary was going to her aunt in the West Country and with Flora, would spend Christmas with our mutual friend

Elsa, Belgian multilingual translator and vicar's wife from the Ecumenical conference. We arrived on Christmas eve, in the midst of hectic preparations for Christmas lunch. The Carol Service from Kings College Cambridge was filling the warm house at top volume, Elsa was stirring a pot and her dignified Belgian mother was conducting with a wooden spoon. Flora, of course, was looking on benignly and not doing much, and the vicar was preparing his sermon in the wood-lined study. It felt like a protective nest. We were grateful for the shelter and the implication that we were free to work out our relationship. We could relax in this sanctuary for the duration of the holidays. That night we stayed up and went to the midnight Mass. French carols were sung, "Minuit Chrêtiens" and "Il est né le Divin Enfant". It could not have been more perfect. Christmas passed with real candles alight on the tree and superb French cooking on the table. We were able to put aside our stress and the dread of parting and simply enjoy being part of a warm family home. Just to be together was bliss.

We went together to Eastbourne where I was engaged to sing at a wedding. We crept into the empty Devonshire Park Language school and marvelled at the marble fireplaces and chandeliers. We visited my little flat and happened to meet my intuitive landlady Rosemary on the stairs. Later she pulled me aside to say "Who was that on the stairs? He is a golden person. Treasure him!"

We heard that we were invited by Lady Astor to Tuesley Manor in Surrey, for New Year's Eve. There was much discussion about what to wear. Flora wore red velvet, Mary, black. I had an orange Thai silk dress and a necklace of orange stones brought by Kieran from South Africa. We were entertained in unaccustomed splendour. Ecumenism had many levels it seemed. Our relationship was once again accepted and we were discreetly placed in rooms with an adjoining door. Bronwyn, Lady Astor was an experienced society hostess well practiced in discretion. We were being given permission to be together in love and integrity. A few days after Christmas Kieran left again. He was still working on delivering the reports of his worldwide mission visits to Chapter meetings in a number of European Capitals, in America and in Canada. This time, when we said goodbye it was not so stressful. We felt that there was still a chance that we would meet again during the next year.

And meet again we did. In the spring he came through London one Saturday en route from Rome. I smuggled him as a guest into the University Womens' Club in South Audley Street of which I was a member. The club was known to residents of the area as the "Hag and Bag" due to the ancient academic members who were seen entering the premises. We were hardly a typical pair of guests. Kieran brought with him a flask of Chianti in its raffia basket and we talked almost all night and drank far too much of the wine. By the time we woke up to go to Mass in the Farm Street Jesuit Church on Sunday morning we both had hangovers and splitting headaches. It was not the most memorable sermon.

Back in Eastbourne I saw an advertisement for a three week Summer course in German at the Hochschule in Vienna. This sounded exciting, and I enquired if Kieran was likely to be in Europe at the time. He was, and could arrange to be in Austria, staying at a monastery for those vacation weeks in the summer. By scraping money together the course was booked and I set off on another long train journey across Europe. I encountered once more the European phenomenon of 'cuchettes' - little fold down shelves in carriages, which looked like drawers left open in a chest, and came with a pillow and a blanket. Passengers of all shapes and sizes eyed each other and arranged themselves on their shelves to sleep and snore the night away. Those three weeks in Vienna were joyous and terrible. For one thing, Kieran met me at the station sporting a piratical black beard. It made him seem like an intimidating stranger. We were ecstatic to be together, and our love was stronger than ever, but at times I was tearful. Kieran felt threatened by my tears, feeling that I was trying to blackmail him out of the priesthood. It was not true. The tears came unbidden. We loved the course and the work. We visited Schoennbrunn Palace where tiny red squirrels put their paws on our shoes to beg for crusts, we went to drink the new wine in the Vienna Woods, and reeled back home on the tram. We were imperiously whistled at by fierce old city wardens for walking on the grass in manicured public parks. We discovered that breakfast in Vienna consisted solely of cake, ate copious quantities of schnitzel and dumplings, took circular trams around the Ring Road, and rode on the giant Ferris wheel in the Prater where Kieran mischievously insisted on rocking the gondola. We attended a reception in the Rathaus for all the summer students. We went for a weekend to the monastery of Rossau outside Vienna where I stayed in the guest quarters and felt extremely unclerical and conspicuous. The time together highlighted both our love and its difficulties but there was no question of the emotional turmoil splitting us apart.

Gravestone of Kieran's parents. Castlerea, Co. Roscommon

Kieran as a baby with elder sisters (1936)

Top left: Pamela as a baby in Australia (1943);
Top right: Pamela schooldays, Australia (1959);
Bottom: Kieran, the young seminarian.

Top: Kieran in Zululand (early 1960s)
Bottom left: Pamela passport photo leaving Australia 1968; Bottom right
Pamela, standing with her back to the Duomo, surrounded by pigeons.

Top left: The Palazzo
Galenga, Universita per
Stranieri Perugia; top
right: Perugia, Corso
Vanucci;

Middle left: Gazing out at
the Etruscan Arch;
middle right: The
winding aqueduct road;

Bottom: The soft blue
seats at the front of the
Aula Magna (Great Hall)

Top: The departure, saying goodbye, January 1969;

Bottom: New Year's Eve, Tuesley Manor, Godalming (1970)

Kieran at the Servite General Chapter 1968

Top left: Siena, blessing the horse before the race;

Top right: Siena;

Middle: Siena, the Palio;

Right: The Church of San Silvestro, Rome

Top: New Year's Eve 1970
(L to R. Flora Glendon Hill, Lady Astor
pouring coffee, Mary Tanner, Pamela).

Left and below: Picnic in Ireland 1977

8
STARTING A COMMUNITY.

I arrived back in England from Vienna with a bad cold, and a cracked rib from violent coughing after swallowing a particularly crumb-covered schnitzel the wrong way. The next move was to Godalming in Surrey, where the new ecumenical adventure was forming under the financial aegis of Lady Astor. The huge Effingham Park venture was proving too isolated, too expensive and too impractical. It would be sold and Lady A had purchased several properties and cottages adjacent to her home, Tuesley Manor by dint, she said, of selling "One of my spare Degas paintings."

A job was advertised at the local library for very little pay. It would involve a two and a half mile walk through the fields to work every day. The route went down a steep hill and then through fields, hedges and allotments. There was a farm belonging to a group of nuns, the Medical Mission Sisters where young women were trained in cold weather agriculture before being sent out to Africa to work in the tropics with local people. Whatever the weather – and it could be freezing – there were often bizarre glimpses of laughing young women wearing white veils pinned back, driving tractors or other farm machinery. Once I saw them tobogganing down a slope. Together with Gillian, a gentle young woman with a dry sense of humour, I volunteered to move into one of the cottages on Lady Astor's estate as pioneer members of this community.

Lady Astor, whom I had met in Switzerland and at the New Year's party, was a tall, beautiful woman who had been a highly regarded fashion model for the House of Balmain

in Paris in her youth, - the Naomi Campbell of her day –
and had married Lord Astor. She had had, she said, a
powerful spiritual experience and was left looking for meaning in her life after the Profumo Affair – when John Profumo, other members of parliament and some Russian spies
were found to be cavorting in the pool with call girls at the
Astor mansion, Cliveden. She was devastated when the
scandal and the subsequent fall of the government led to
her being shunned by her previous aristocratic friends and
she retreated to a manor house deep in the lanes of Surrey.
Tuesley Manor was a vast rambling 15th century stone
house with many outbuildings. It was furnished luxuriously
with silk curtains and Toile de Jouy. Lady Astor herself, tall
and gaunt was still very beautiful, very glamorous, very rich,
and very much the chatelaine. She swooped around in
sables, long gowns and cloaks, and was wont to receive visitors in her silk draped four poster bed surrounded by goat-
skin rugs. She could be surprisingly parsimonious at times.
Magnificent old red wines from the cellar had to be drunk
willy nilly at dinner if they were in danger of turning to vin-
egar. There was a fine rage one morning because the cat
had licked the butter. While very regal and imperious, there
was a sense that somewhere beneath the elegant exterior
there was a panic stricken child who could sometimes appear unexpectedly. She was wont to make cutting remarks,
which she expected others to forget as quickly as she did.
One of those unfortunate people born without a sense of
humour, she could laugh with others, but never seemed sure
why. The lady appeared to favour the men who visited Tuesley Manor over the women, and was charm itself to visiting
priests. And there were many, Jesuits, Dominicans, Bene-
dictines, White Fathers. Later on, as the community developed, Lady A had a tendency to make visitations with
rich friends from London to parade us as "My Community". But that was for the future.

Gillian and I moved into a small cottage with rampant ivy-patterned wallpaper and no central heating. We had little furniture but managed to acquire a few essential chairs and tables second hand. One day Gillian went to a jumble sale and brought back a slightly threadbare Indian style carpet rolled up on her bicycle. We acquired a very rusty and tarnished brass jardinière and spent hours cleaning it with tomato sauce. We experimented with vegetarian curry. We were full of good intentions. But first we had to make a living. My library job would keep me afloat – just. Gillian saw a likely advertisement for a draughtsman position in the nearby town of Guildford. There was a postal strike so she waylaid the dustcart and persuaded the dustman to post her letter of application. Soon others turned up to join us. Bronwyn hired a young, handsome and very trendy cook called Phillip, who wore purple velvet flares from Carnaby Street, and he came along with three friends to inhabit the cottage next door. A young couple, plus a single Mother with an angelic baby. Philip cooked sporadically for Lady Astor, but fell out of favour when he fell in love with Angie, the single mother and moved in with her. The rest of that group seemed to have no visible means of support, nor did they have any spiritual aspirations.

"Oh!' Said Lady A, airily, with an expansive hand gesture, "We must be ready to take in waifs and strays".

A kind and gentle elderly woman called Freda turned up to manage Quarry Cottage, the big house which was destined to be the heart of the community, and we waited for further developments. An entire American family with five children appeared, – at least this time Bob Balkam, the husband and father was prepared to put energy into organising events although his very dramatic wife, Lauren, having taught her children to run the house, seemed to spend a great deal of time sitting around with a cigarette in her

120

hand, expounding esoteric and incomprehensible spiritual theories.

As the weeks and months went by, the weather became colder, and with the leadership of Bob and a very handsome young French priest called Roger Labonté, charismatic prayer meetings began to happen in Quarry Cottage on a Friday night. The singing was beautiful, and some people spoke in tongues, a phenomenon called glossolalia, which seemed to be freeing. The meetings began in a small way, but rapidly increased as Lady A invited everyone she met. She then decided that giving refreshments to all these people would be far too expensive, so gigantic packets of cornflakes were purchased and the crowds were regaled with cornflakes and milk after their prayerful exertions. As the meetings grew larger and larger, Gillian and I began to feel like refugees from the crowds.

In October, Kieran made his final visit to London. He was very keen to go with me to see Oscar Köllerstrom. In his mind was the idea that this would "help" me in some way. I was not so sure I wanted to be "helped". We went to London on a cold and foggy evening and Kieran, who was expecting the session to be about "helping" Pamela, rapidly found that it was deflected to being about himself. It evolved into a very searching session. After a long discussion Kieran found himself backed into a corner where he was forced to look clearly at our relationship, and to make a committed decision one way or another. He came down on the side of honesty, and from his deepest integrity had to say-

"Yes" he did want to remain a priest, and "Yes", he did want to return to Africa permanently.

To me this was not unexpected. After all, it was how I had seen our relationship from the beginning, painful though it was. I knew he had taken his vows of poverty, chastity and obedience with great seriousness and being the man of integrity that he was, could not see himself breaking them. Curiously, my instant and abiding reaction was one of enormous relief that this truth was now out in the open. Yes, we loved each other and at the same time yes this was what he wanted. At the end of the session we went out of the house and down the illuminated path and I found myself humming a tune despite the emotional pain. All the way home, throughout a warming meal in a "Chelsea Kitchen" restaurant it was perfectly possible to make loving replies to everything that was said. I felt no resentment and no desire for any kind of regret or recriminations. We loved each other with all our hearts and souls but I had never expected him to marry me.

Only on the train home did I realise that at each difficult moment I had been raising my eyes inwardly and looking at the image of a most beautiful crucifix. I had never seen one like it before, although it had some similarities to the Franciscan crucifix of San Damiano. It seemed to be made of dark gold metal with a ridge around it, and was inlaid with the most vivid scarlet enamel imaginable. The central figure placed, but not visibly nailed on the cross was not the usual figure, but a very white human figure neither male nor female and the whole picture was illuminated with an extraordinarily bright light, between white and gold. The image had been there all during the difficult conversation as a support. I cannot imagine how I would have reacted had it not been there.

The next day, visiting Mary at a chapel in Kent, I looked up and saw an unusual hollow iron sculpture, a cross. Where the figure would have been there was air and space and it was silhouetted against a vivid red sunset sky, like a reminder.

When Kieran left the day after that it was a cold, biting, day, the iron-grey skies threatening snow. I took him to Heathrow airport. He hated prolonged farewells and we said a long, difficult and painful goodbye. The plane was late and we both profoundly wished that boarding would be called. I think we were both glad when it was done and he turned and strode through the departure gates with his dear uneven, loping stride.

I caught the airport bus back into central London and went for a singing lesson. Cruelly, the first song to sing that day was

"How beautiful are the feet of them that preach the gospel of peace," from Handel's Messiah.

After that life went on, although the light had dimmed. The library work was boring and unchallenging but very physically tiring, coupled with the long walk back and forth from the town in all weathers.

The relationships in the community waxed and waned depending on who Lady A invited to join. People came and went, not always amicably. Real leadership seemed to have evaporated. Mary was given a small flat in a stable courtyard and lived a quiet hermit life, counselling those who wanted to see her. Flora had had a kind of breakdown due to exhaustion and had gone to stay with Elsa in Essex. We were asked not to visit her. At one stage Lady A decided she wanted to build a chapel and we were all summoned to work with shovels and cement mixers. The stresses and strains and petty conflicts in the community began to resemble the dysfunctional community depicted in "The Bell" by Iris Murdoch. Although the lofty aim was to allow the Holy Spirit to lead and guide in all things, it seemed that the Holy Spirit required a modicum of common sense and a bit of discipline to be applied. It was not proving to be so easy to weld a very disparate group together, without strong leadership and clearly stated aims. In default of moderation and rules, the community began to be ruled by whoever had the strongest neuroses. And to be honest, that person was probably Lady A. The writing was on the wall. This community was fragmenting.

Kieran's letters had been coming at less regular intervals. In December an envelope with his dear beetle track writing arrived. I fell on it eagerly and opened it. I read that from then on he would no longer write. He could not continue the correspondence and felt that our relationship had to stop completely. While I knew that he was writing from the depths of his integrity, it was a shock. That was that, then. There was no chance of being Clare to his Francis, let alone Heloise to his Abelard. I had seen myself as the lifelong contemplative side of his active vocation and other grand things. It was over. I would never again see the joy on his face as he walked towards me, never again hear his warm laughing voice as he called me "La mia biondina!" (My little blonde).

Despite living in a community supposedly based on love there was no-one to talk to except my analyst and although I phoned him to tell him he did not waste time on emotion. I lay down by the cold fireplace and cried for a long time. Then I burned the letter and wrote a poem.

THE LETTER.

I gently placed the letter in the flame
And watched it as the fire caressed it round.
From edge to death resisting heart it came
A tortured victim writhing without sound.

White paper soon is burnt and eaten whole
As blow-able as a char of thistledown,
While I in weary worship knelt before
A desiccated ghost of written soul.

Nothing can restore black ash to white
Replace a soul into its broken shell,
No-one can recapture time to write
The old desires or pleas or cast a spell
To exorcise the fears or ease the pain.
Now, heart my phoenix, can you rise again?

9

A BLEAK SPACE BARE OF APPLES

There was still work to go to, the long freezing walks to and from the library, still day to day life in the community to attend to, still singing lessons once a week, although these became less spontaneous and more difficult, still sessions with Mr Köllerstrom to attend. It was December 1970, and Christmas was coming. Always a lover of everything sparkly and Christmassy, I wanted nothing to do with it and went to Paris to stay in a small Left Bank hotel, slept most of Christmas Day and wandered alone along the Seine.

The love and the loss was always with me wherever I went. I awoke every morning and for a moment the world would seem normal until bleak reality crashed in again. Life had lost its meaning. Having given myself heart and soul to the relationship with Kieran I had no desire to reclaim what had been given away. Who was the person I had been? And how to take back that person? I didn't even want to find her again. I had been completely prepared to give the rest of my life to this relationship, and to sublimate our passion in love, letters, prayer and support. What was left, now that life had to be lived for myself alone seemed very poor and not worth having. Was there anything left? I wrote at the time-

"These weeks I have shed so many tears of grief for the loss of Kieran. Is it possible that one can be so maimed that, like an animal caught in a road accident, the only thing for a humane bystander to say is "Put it out of its misery".

Going to a local Doctor for antidepressants I was told summarily that I would probably not recover for two years. It was hardly helpful. One day I went in to a London hairdressers and demanded to have all my hair cut off, ordered an Italian meal and left without eating it, and unintentionally "shoplifted" several pieces of music from Foyles bookshop. I dyed my hair red for a while and wore only masculine clothes. All good psychoanalytical material.

In the new year Mr Köllerstrom announced one day that I was in danger of turning into an iceberg if I did not go out and meet some men. I had no desire to do so but obediently enrolled in a computer dating organisation called Dateline. For a small fee, one filled in a form with copious personal details and somewhere an enormous computer the size of a room chewed up the data and matched applicants up with members of the opposite sex who would supposedly be compatible.

There followed a bizarre period of meeting various men, usually on Victoria Station with or without a red carnation in their buttonholes or carrying a copy of The Times. I had no conception that this might be a dangerous pursuit – danger had never really entered into my calculations and fortunately none of them proved to be murderers, rapists or swindlers- (not that I had anything to swindle.) One problem was that I felt each of us, on meeting, was summing up the other to try and discern why this person had to resort to Dateline to meet a prospective partner. What was wrong with them? There was John, a sweet natured blonde engineer who was painfully shy and had a pronounced stammer, Pete who rode a motorbike, wore leathers and expected me to go for hair-raising rides with him, Anthony, a wealthy antiques dealer from Ascot who couldn't bear to be touched and sat on the opposite side of the room, (why did he want to meet a woman I wondered?) and another chap whose name I have forgotten who lived in Harrow on the Hill, who made tea and spent an entire afternoon lecturing me on his theory that Ancient Egyptians had migrated to South America who knows when and had transformed themselves into the Inca or was it the Aztec civilisation. It was becoming obvious that this was not going to work.

Mr Köllerstrom then suggested enrolling in "Katherine Allen's Marriage Bureau". This involved still more elaborate form filling and an interview with the stately and formally dressed owner of the bureau. The subsequent meetings were all with more affluent gentlemen – the fee was substantial – who were, if possible even more inarticulate, stiff and boring than the Dateline crop. Having spent hours waiting outside the Cumberland Hotel near Marble Arch for some kind of American businessman, I found myself fighting off the attentions of an amorous Turk who claimed to be stupendously endowed, and decided this was not for me.

Then the library suddenly proved more interesting. I was up a ladder replacing books, wearing a miniskirt, as we did in those days, when a large, muscular man with a spade shaped beard walked in, and asked where he could find books on tropical diseases to research a novel he was writing on the Spanish Conquistador Alva Nunez Cabeza de Vaca. I directed him to the correct place and he found what he wanted.

Going back to Tuesley Manor that evening, I found gentle little Freda, our house – mother all agog and twittering about a speaker who had addressed the local Women's Institute. He was a big bearded chap, she said and he came from some institute called Esalen in America where they did weird things and he said they all ought to take off their clothes and have saunas together. This sounded more interesting than usual, for Godalming, and I suspected it might be my man from the library. The following Friday he turned up at the weekly prayer meeting, invited, of course by Lady A. He took part unobtrusively in the proceedings with one eyebrow raised, and came into the cottage next door where we carried out a kind of unspoken flirtation by alternately petting a kitten all evening.

Daniel Panger and I formed a very brief relationship. He was fresh from the campus in Berkeley, California, and had just done a year at the Esalen Institute, headquarters of the Human Potential Movement. He had become a Unitarian Minister, largely because he saw it as a way of talking about subjects he considered important. Bizarrely he was in genteel Godalming on a summer exchange with the local Minister and lived in a tiny manse in the middle of a graveyard. An interesting place for an assignation. Among the things he considered important was Humanistic Psychology. The whole concept of Encounter Groups was new to England at the time and was being pioneered in London by alternative organisations such as Quaesitor, and Kaleidoscope operating in a couple of disused or condemned houses in less than salubrious areas. Talking to Daniel I realised that this might be a way to get through to the next stage of growth. Here was a person who was a brilliant writer and a challenging conversationalist. No statement got past him if it had the slightest taint of dishonesty. There was no room for falsity, though plenty of room for spirituality in the widest sense. I was so interested that I resolved to go to London to become involved in the Humanistic Psychology movement for myself.

Daniel returned to the United States and I linked up with a second bearded visitor to the community, six foot seven Bob, who was far less sure of himself, but up for a bit of fun. Mr Kollerstrom was, I think approving that I had now admitted male company into my life, but very suspicious of Humanistic psychology. It became obvious that my time in the Ecumenical community was drawing to a close. It was becoming claustrophobic. Gillian and I, despite our auspicious start were having our differences, due to issues with house tidiness and chores, as well as a boyfriend who could not decide which one of us he was interested in. In frustration, one night I threw a goblet we had bought as a symbol of our partnership against the wall. It refused to break – a good predictor of our friendship which has survived a lifetime. I decided to leave and go to London. And having decided to come to some understanding of myself with regard to men and sexuality, it didn't seem appropriate to be masquerading any longer as a good catholic virgin.

I told Lady A I was leaving, and offered to come back to the community to help during weekends. She tossed her head and said:

"We're not a hotel you know! Don't bother!"

So that was that. The break was made. With the help of Bob, my tall, bearded friend, I transported my goods to London, to a flat share in Victoria.

(I would not see Lady A again for more than ten years when one day, I spotted her at the top of an Escalator in the elegant department store, Fenwicks, in Bond Street. By then life had changed. I was a more confident person, used to authority and far better dressed. We spoke briefly. She waved a hand vaguely and said "I believe you have been *abroad*"– that portmanteau term that the upper classes like to use to dismiss the rest of the world. To the end of her life she referred to "her" Community.)

Back in 1970 I applied for "supply teaching" in London, – a system whereby teachers are called in at a moment's notice to substitute for absences in the state schools. It lasted one day. The outsize classes operated at the volume of a steady scream, the students had no interest in learning and spent the entire day throwing missiles at each other and abusing the teachers. Life was too short for this. I did not go back but instead began work in Stamford, Lincolnshire at something called a Girls' Direct Grant school, teaching English and living as an assistant housemistress. It was a glimpse into another side of the English school system. The girls were almost all highly motivated and keen. Some were fee-paying and some were not. The boarding system worked well although as a point of honour they all pretended to hate the food. I was working under an enlightened and dedicated head of the English Department. "You can have any books you want, – all I ask is that the pupils should enjoy learning, love reading and write well," she said. It was a license to have fun, and the pupils responded.

Stamford itself was picturesque, with a silhouette of church towers, full of pale stone houses built in the 17th and 18th Centuries. Walking down the steep street from the school, one reached the George Inn, a coaching Inn where horses used to be changed on their way north, and where there was still the stump of an ancient mulberry tree reputed to have been planted by Huguenot weavers. After crossing the river Nene and the water meadows the town and its squares appeared, hosting once a week the modern descendent of the ancient cloth market, and once a year, the funfair, where dignified Stamford residents could be seen taking fairground rides or solemnly walking the wobbly 'cakewalk' with their shopping bags in their hands. Beyond the Stamford High School was the Elizabethan Burghley House, magical with its forest of pointed towers and turrets, a place to explore, to walk in the park, to watch baby rabbits or sniff grasses. It was said that it took at least fifteen years in Stamford before one could expect to be accepted as a resident, – or even spoken to, and this I could believe, since all of the houses in the town presented unforgiving stony-faced walls to the street. It was hard to imagine how people would meet each other. That was not a problem however since there was plenty of life going on in the school, and even more in "The Nuns" – the school boarding house where I was a 'Deputy House Mistress' "but in reality more of a big sister. I would sit on the floor listening to pop opera with the sixth formers, while younger classes felt free to ask how to hold a midnight feast and would I please keep the Matron occupied while they did so.

There began a period of contrasts. During the week I was a correct, well dressed and hard-working schoolmistress, still going to London on every second Friday for therapy and a singing lesson. But during many weekends I would enrol in a Growth Movement workshop that seemed interesting or exciting. Group leaders were brought from American Human Potential centres such as Esalen in California, – pioneers such as Bill Schutz, and Jay Stattman, Jorge Rosner and Richard Olney. Donning jeans and T shirt we would join a group sitting on cushions to participate in some kind of growth event. Theory and analysis was discouraged and in that environment psychoanalysis and 'talking therapies' were treated as dirty words. What theory there was was based on the work of Abraham Maslow, Carl Rogers and Fritz Perls whose writings we all read with excitement. Arthur Janov's book The Primal Scream was in all of our bookshelves. The emphasis was on touch, experience, emotion and honesty. People might be facing their imaginary parents or partners and shouting at them as they beat cushions to exorcise old traumas, it might be a Gestalt Dream workshop, a Bio-Energetics workshop of breathing and exercises, a weekend of running, a workshop bases on the Psychosynthesis of Roberto Assagioli, or once, a powerful 48 hour nude intensive run by Denny and Leida Yuson, therapists from Synanon, the New York drug rehabilitation centre, where participants had only a few hours' sleep but where the heightened state of awareness intensified and accelerated emotional break throughs. Catharsis and abreaction were the way forward in these experiential groups, whatever the techniques were that might be employed. The rewards were accelerated and intense. Mr Kollerstrom was at first alarmed by these activities but gradually realised that these rapid and extreme periods of learning and development were being integrated by the regular sessions with him. It was a profitable and exciting period.

It felt necessary to throw myself into growth. There were still periods of depression when it was only just possible to force myself to breathe and look at a sunset, and times when I wanted to lock myself away or die. But the job precluded this. Kieran had removed himself from my life. There was no prospect of ever seeing him again, – he had made that clear in his letter. He had washed his hands of me. But his image remained burned on the retina of my mind, filing my heart, overshadowing all other relationships and obliterating them.

I began to have a series of brief encounters. It would often be with the group workshop leader. There was Jorge who was from California and wore floral shirts, white trousers and turquoise jewellery, Dick, who was a slightly dishevelled and sensitive poet and led an illuminating Gestalt Dream workshop, Barry, a tough New Yorker who believed in cutting through pretence, wore cowboy boots, and liked fine dining – sensitive young Pete, a leader- in-training in hippy gear who liked to walk all over London, and a number of others. Whoever it was, it would certainly be a brief conjunction with no commitment and I would be left high and dry very quickly – a sure way of repeating Kieran's departure over and over again. But I no longer expected commitment from anyone. On the other hand, in such weekend workshops, intense relationships are accelerated and every connection had its mutual value. From each experience much was learned on both sides and it was well understood that they were liaisons with no strings attached. In this inching towards psychological stability there was a lot of mutual respect and honesty and each quantum leap was seen and examined in the light of the ongoing therapy with my experienced and unflinching old analyst.

During this period of 'laboratory experience' it seemed necessary to take a break from the previous spiritual traject- ory. Rather as if over my shoulder I had to say:

"Hold on there, God, I just have to go and do other things for a while".

In other circumstances it might and should have been possible to see that all of life is one whole and that sexuality is as essential to the divine creative plan as anything else, perhaps more so than many pious practices. As it was, I knew no-one at the time who was mature enough to have a foot in both camps and to see the whole picture. But any pretence of piety was over, and life was about facing old pat- terns and becoming whole.

As part of the search for what would come next in life I went on a brief trawl through the fringe world of fortune telling. It began with a gypsy on Hampstead Heath who told me I would meet the man of my dreams but would have to give up another relationship first – an older man. As there was no other relationship at the time I filed this away for the present. An Astrologer did a hugely complicated reading which gave a lot of character hints and mentioned writing and diplomacy which was a field I knew nothing about and had never had any curiosity to investigate. I had a palm reading with a renowned palmist called Mir Bashir. His pre- dictions were extraordinarily detailed. If they were accurate I would travel widely, become more comfortable financially, end my life back in Australia, become involved in psycho- logy or medicine, would marry and have the possibility of two children if I wished. Mrs Bates, a tarot card reader in West London was the most amazing of all. She predicted that in summer – August, I would meet the perfect man. She saw him in Africa surrounded by African people. He would be completely certain of what he wanted when he arrived and would be driving a long blue car. He would be involved in war zones and would fly about in a lot of small planes, and there would be a large gift of money coming my way before the marriage. Kieran obviously did not enter my mind since obviously he had gone and would never return.

The next suitor from the Marriage Bureau was a small, neat gentleman from Kenya. I had a beauty treatment before meeting him and wore my best black velvet jacket for the lunch. He was, sadly as disappointing as all the rest. It seemed that Tarot card readers can see months but are rather hazy about which year things might happen.

After two years in Lincolnshire, I returned to London hoping to get a place at University and a grant to study psychology. A flat in West Kensington, a small place with very thin walls and very noisy neighbours was shared with an Australian friend, Sue. We would halve the rental, she would live there and I would return at weekends and holidays. Unfortunately, like many such arrangements, it began to fray at the edges. Sue was a sensitive soul, and compulsively clean. She would snatch plates away to wash and dry them again, and spent her days obsessively polishing the flat. She was extremely beautiful with long, luxuriant strawberry blonde hair, but was terrified lest anyone should see her without her full makeup and false eyelashes which she even wore to bed. I was certainly not up to her standards and we eventually parted company. A one roomed flat became available in Hampstead, overlooking the Heath. I thankfully accepted it and moved there when the term ended in Stamford. The flat was lofty and looked out into trees. I loved it. It had green walls and a strawberry pink ceiling – and oddly, a bath in the kitchen which could lead to some sybaritic meals. Hampstead was a pretty, arty area with much to explore, and acres of Heath to enjoy. The psychology grant was refused but I looked forward to a pleasant summer while looking for employment.

During that summer of 1973, still in search of adventure, I bought copies of the alternative "Time Out" magazine and looked at advertisements in the Lonely Hearts columns. This horrified Mr Kollerstrom, who expected all kinds of criminals and perverts to be advertising in such a publication. Perhaps he might have trusted the "New Statesman" more. One advertiser seemed more interesting than the others, written by a lover of the outdoors, of opera and concerts, in particular Benjamin Britten and Mahler. I was not particularly enamoured of either but was struck by the literary style of the paragraph. We arranged to meet on Hampstead Heath and he said he would be "wearing a bull terrier". Not quite sure what this was I donned my jeans with the butterfly patch on the bum and went out looking for a man with some kind of dog. He proved to be an ex-army major. I was by then aged 30. He was 55. Initially he claimed to be 50.

His name was Richard. He was short, trim and fit, with an unappealing pudding basin haircut, and a face that could look rather sour. He slightly resembled the painting of the young King George III by Thomas Lawrence. He had pets – an enchanting and gentle English Bull Terrier called Ginta, and a feisty Siamese cat, called Soandso, or Pud, a flat full of exotic curios from his travels, a mastery of cooking, an appetite for endless operas and concerts, and romantic imagination displayed in little gifts at my door. He produced flowers, plans for country escapades, magical birthdays and wonderful Christmases with piles of presents and sparkling balls tied to trees in the snow. He was likely to arrive carrying a bouquet in one hand and a creme brûlée in the other. I remember being collected at 3 am for a drive through the night so that we could see sunrise over Stonehenge and have breakfast in Bath. We went to every opera in London – one year we queued all night for a Wagner opera at Covent Garden (and were too tired to enjoy it) and traipsed to Birmingham and Bristol in full evening dress to complete not one but two Ring Cycles.

At the beginning it seemed that I had found the ideal partner and I was fascinated. This was a man with experience of the world, access to culture and a life story beyond anything I had met. Few young women could resist such a courtship. Life with Richard was a feast of art, music and indulgence. He was a brilliant writer and poet, and a talented artist, with a clever sense of humour. I settled myself in to enjoy an exciting life full of treats.

But as time went on, flaws appeared. Although he may well have believed he was genuinely devoted, he was also possessive, prone to anxiety attacks and something of an emotional sadist. He was damaged by his childhood in boarding school, his absentee parents – his father was a naval doctor – and by his wartime experiences as a Chindit fighting in the jungles of Burma. He was prone to sudden and devastating mood changes. I would find that, without warning, when things seemed sunny between us, a tornado would erupt. Asked why he was angry he would shout back with fury "I'm not angry!" If he failed to spot me in a secluded corner of a pub I would be accused of "Deliberately hiding". A bad driver, a noise in a theatre or a pneumatic drill that disturbed him could reduce him to blind fury. I began to dread being out with him since if he found someone's behaviour rude or offensive he had no qualms about making a scene. Sometimes his tirades and grievances only seemed to be assuaged when he had reduced me to tears. Today, it might be called Coercive Control. Back then I just thought that relationships could be very hard work.

In some ways the experience paralleled my relationship with my mother. Both wanted to be loving but expressed that desire by control. It can be difficult not to fall back into earlier traps. When love is twinned with control in our childhood, we can find it difficult to do without that pairing in later life. It can take long and conscious inner work to break such patterns. And although I was engaged in that inner

137

work, it was not completed. Richard could change from the
suitor of dreams to a hurt and petulant child. I set out to
"help" him and to save his soul – always a mistake.

Mr Köllerstrom came as near as an analyst can to losing
his cool about the relationship, and several times pleaded
with me to end it at all costs, saying that this was not love,
but obsession. I tried, but Richard had a most curious
power. In an early attempt to end the relationship I screwed
up courage and made the break, leaving London, to stay
with friends in the country for a week. On the morning I
decided to leave, I wept and his Siamese cat, Pud, licked
away my tears. On return from the country, I was walking
up Parliament Hill towards my flat in the early evening. The
door of a nearby house opened, and the powerful aroma of
the incense that Richard always burned wafted out. At the
same moment I heard a car horn and turned to find that
Richard had materialised, pulling up behind me, tearful,
pleading and forgiving. I always found myself returning to
him and seemed unable to face life alone, even though what
he offered was neurotic interdependency. When I developed
pneumonia he cared for me, cooking little delicacies, bringing his dog and his siamese cat to keep me company. His
kindness could be as immense as his irrational cruelty. For
four years I was a doll and plaything of someone I certainly
did not love and did not always like, but I could be manipu-
lated into a semblance of loving behaviour through fear, or
treats or pity. It was a very lessening relationship, so different
from the memory of how much Kieran and I had increased
each other when we were together. It was very telling that
none of my friends liked Richard. I would not have wanted
to introduce him to my parents nor could I envisage marry-
ing him. I would not have wanted to bear his child. And yet
it seemed impossible to break free. The operas, the concerts,
the mushroom gathering and camping, the flowers, the pic-

nics, the moonlight rambles and the tantrums – all continued to ensnare me.

One activity which Richard was keen to do together was Transcendental meditation which was sweeping London. I finally agreed to meet blonde Giselle in Kensington who had initiated him into the system, saved up my contribution to the organisation and went along to receive my TM mantra. To sink back into silence and meditation felt like coming home. It should not have been a surprise.

From that time I knew I needed to reactivate some kind of spiritual life. I had not been to church for some years but I began to meditate and pray again. Living in close contact with Richard this was difficult, even though we did not live together. He became jealous of any activity I attended alone, and if I took him to any kind of service or meeting it was sure to be embarrassingly bad. But I persisted, even attending a small house church in North London with my friend Gillian, where it appeared that the thing to do was to get re-baptised in the bath wearing a long white robe. Apart from near drowning it did not seem to have any great effect. However, I did go to a church weekend with the same group in Dorset. Somewhere during the evening I heard the words "You shall have your heart's desire", a common enough Biblical-sounding quote – and yet it struck me to the heart, as though the words were meant specifically for me. But the only heart's desire I had was for Kieran – and that was impossible.

Somewhere during that year,1975, I left Mr Köllerstrom. We had become friendly and he was somewhat taken aback when I left though later we established a good relationship and he was pleased that I no longer felt the need of his sessions. I began some creative activities, – re-commenced singing, bought a Celtic harp and began to take lessons and to sing Irish and Scottish folksongs, learned to spin and weave, and threw myself into the joys of keeping tropical fish.

Winters in London were hard. Cold, dark, rainy and slushy underfoot. Christmas was bearable but the aftermath was depressing. With a good friend, Mary Dwyer, from Canada, an escape was planned with a small travel company which specialised in long weekends in various capital cities. Mary wanted to go to Dublin. I resisted, not wanting to be reminded of Kieran. But she was determined to investigate her Irish ancestry. Dublin exceeded our expectations. From the moment we set foot in the city the people delighted us with their friendliness and humour.

Our Bed and Breakfast in Clontarf was owned by garrulous Mrs Murphy who, when I commented on the smell of bacon frying for breakfast, replied:

"Yes, cuts you to the heart doesn't it!"

When Mary tripped entering a bus the driver remarked:

"Try and keep her off the hard stuff now won't you!"

We loved the National Museum with its ancient treasures rescued from peat bogs, we loved Trinity College and the medieval Celtic harp, we loved the folk music concert we discovered. We were amused at the appalled reaction when we accidentally trespassed into what was apparently a sacred males – only pub. The expressions were so scandalised that we fantasised remarks like "Paddy do you think they're whores?" We were fascinated to observe the physical types in the streets – a mixture of leprechauns and stunningly handsome black-haired Irishmen. I had expected to be emotionally seared by being in Ireland, Kieran's country, but found instead that it was like being enclosed in a warm hug. I could only feel embraced by his presence in these places.

The following year, we went to Rome. Once again I resisted strongly until the bookings were actually made. But

140

Mary was so keen to see the Eternal City it was hard to deny her. It became a pilgrimage. Visiting the Servite Monastery and church of San Marcello, San Silvestro where I had been received into the Church, The Borghese Gardens when we had talked until midnight, The Pantheon and the dancing fountains of Piazza Navona. We bought beautiful fine gloves in a tiny shop in the Corso, ate artichokes in the Piazza della Tartaruga with the little fountain supported by turtles, bought panini and ate them in the sun near St Peters. Once again, facing the ghosts was not painful but like being surrounded with loving memories.

It seemed that life was becoming interesting, creative and bearable but on returning to London, the cleft stick of the relationship with Richard was still ongoing. But despite all the positive signs, I became truly panic stricken when Richard proposed marriage and suggested a trip to the Welsh border to look at a cottage for sale. I would have been his third wife. That did not seem to me to augur well. I went with him, in mental turmoil as to how I could escape his plans.

10

LIFE THAT STIRS AND GROWS

Going back in time, while all these events were happening, in early 1975 I had heard through the ecumenical grapevine, via gentle little Father Gerry Corr and Flora, that Kieran had had a bad car accident in Africa and had, or had almost lost a leg. This had happened some time ago and he was apparently going to America for physiotherapy and a study course. I was aghast at this news, visualising his tall, beautiful, athletic body so mutilated. I wrote a very formal get-well letter via the mission address, and later heard that on his way through London he had contacted the old Community in Surrey hoping to see Lady Astor. This tested my Christian charity considerably, but then, why should he visit me? We had parted and we would never meet again. He had broken off all contact.

Nothing further was heard until the following year, the second year of fulfilling and lively work in the Overseas Scholarship section of the British Council. It was the most enjoyable job I had ever had. Far from finding office work boring I found that I enjoyed clearing my desk, mastering the complex procedures, and solving the daily problems encountered in planning and supervising the studies of postgraduate students in varied fields, from dozens of different countries. I loved meeting them. It was satisfying when they succeeded and highly diverting at times when cultural misunderstandings resulted in hilarious situations. Students misunderstood directions, spent vast amounts of money they didn't have, and ended up in remote parts of England where they shouldn't be and had to be rescued. The schol-

142

arship department was composed of a large number of graduates of approximately similar ages and the company was stimulating. After work the operas, concerts, picnics, with Richard, the dog walks and emotional blackmail all continued. Summer 1976 was the hottest Britain had experienced for 350 years. The days dawned, blue and scorching. There were water restrictions in London and we were exhorted to "Save water, bath with a friend!" Trees were dying in the streets and we saved our used water to rescue them. Life in Hampstead began after work with summer picnics and late nights cooling off on the Heath. It was the last days of alternative dressing and it was a joy to don a flowing skirt, T shirt and sandals and stride out to catch an early morning bus in warm sunshine.

Suddenly, in this atmosphere of unaccustomed summer warmth and happiness, I heard, via the same grapevine, that Kieran was again in Europe, after studies in America. This time he was in Ireland. I had been going through a phase of:

"If only I could get rid of Kieran's ghost I might be able to be happy with Richard, or someone else".

And it cannot have been comfortable for Richard to live with a woman with an unresolved past of which he was aware, although we never discussed Kieran.

I obtained the phone number of the Servites in Dublin and phoned one sunny Saturday morning in the summer. The plan was simply to ask how he was and to clear the air. To my complete astonishment Kieran was the only person in the monastery at the time and it was he who answered the phone. He was as surprised as I was and was initially defensive saying, ungallantly-

"You're just trying to start things up again."

I assured him I was not, quite the opposite, and that I was just ringing to enquire after his welfare. By the end of the

143

call I could hear from his voice that he still had warm feelings for me. We parted amicably with no particular intention of keeping in touch but a tenuous bridge was made. Just a couple of planks floating in mid-air with no hand-rails.

The result was surprising. I found that my reaction was to kneel down and say, as I did so many years ago in Perth, "Thy will be Done", over and over again. And once again calm descended. When I stood up and went to the local Camden market I was singing to myself quite happily in the sunshine, not at all depressed.

After much thought I eventually wrote an unemotional short note, telling Kieran something of my activities, and suggesting that if he felt like it we might correspond occasionally on a friendly basis. I enclosed my contact details.

In September I received a reply from Ubombo in Zululand. He explained that he had come through London in July and had thought of visiting the community in Godalming and Lady A but that she was going away. He had then telephoned my flat and office to be told that I too was on holiday. In fact I had been in Malonne in Belgium at another International Ecumenical conference, this time singing and playing the harp and once more enjoying the exciting atmosphere of community that these conferences always engendered. Despite all the men I had dated, and embroiled in the relationship with Richard, the songs I chose to sing with the harp were traditional laments that moved the audience to tears. "Shule Shule Shule Agra" - "Only death can ease my woe, since the lad of my heart from me did go". "The Lass from the Low Countree", and that heartbreaking song of Delius, "Twilight Fancies" - "What is it I long for, What is it I long for? God help me, she cried. And the sun went down, and the sun went down". Whatever was happening on the surface of life, in my heart he was always there.

Kieran wrote that he had spent a year in San Francisco, recovering from his accident and learning to walk again without a limp, while doing an intensive course at the University of Berkeley's 'Institute for Spirituality and Worship". He was now back doing mission work, camping out at outstations every weekend, attending meetings and running courses and retreats during the week. He asked me to write again and signed off demurely "Much love in Christ".

Reading the letter my heart lightened and lifted in a way it had not done for five years. I remember giving much thought to replying, and finally sitting down at the typewriter in October with a feeling of "Well, here goes!" I told him how happy I was to hear from him and something of who I had become and what I was doing. Curiously, although I would never discuss Kieran with Richard, I openly shared with Kieran where that relationship was going, or not going. I asked if he had a photograph of himself.

Christmas 1976 was magical, Richard lit my flat with lights and a Christmas tree in the window, which gave joy when I saw it on the way back from work. There were balloons and presents galore for everyone, including the pets – even the fish. He bought a polished toboggan from Harrods and we slid down Parliament Hill in the moonlight with Ginta the bull terrier, and Pud, the Siamese cat whose frightful yowling curses had best go unrecorded.

After Christmas, my obsessively tidy Australian friend Sue had a bad mental breakdown. It might have been predicted. She disappeared for some time and I then tracked her down at a maximum-security mental institution north of London. I rang Mr Kollerstrom's number to see if he could give some advice. He had died in February. His beautiful ballet dancer wife Bridget who had trained in therapy, was counselling his clients to help them to cope with the loss. I went to see her.

It had been a cold, hard winter. In February there was another letter from Kieran. This time he was writing from the Servite mission by the sea where he had been sent to recuperate from illness and overwork. He spoke about his efforts to apply some of the inspirational new ideas he had learned in Berkeley, California. He had left one course called "Spirituality and Worship" because he found the lecturer anti-feminist and and changed to a course on "Spiritual Direction." This, he hoped, would help him in his work giving retreats throughout South Africa for which he was becoming well known and much in demand. Back in Zululand, he was running himself ragged trying to revive tired outstations which had been neglected while he was away. He had worked himself to a standstill, and had come down with a variety of fevers, tried to go back too soon and collapsed again. He was pondering whether mission work in South Africa had any future, wondering if his forte was in giving retreats after the exciting and intensive course he had done in California, but at the same time seeing the necessity of training African catechists and priests to take over the African Church which he had always seen as the ultimate aim. He had written a complete training programme in Zulu and was setting about single-handed to do this work. He sounded tired, convalescent, but characteristically enthusiastic.

This time the letter ended: "Be good Pam, and do write again." And in VERY small writing, at the bottom, as if hoping not to be seen,

"I do love you, Kieran."

I filed the letter away, buoyed up by that small admission, slipped in, sotto voce, on the last line. Kieran was still deep in his priestly duties and overworking with dedication but there was a small thread of relationship there. I would have been content with that.

146

In late May 1977 another letter arrived in the letterbox in Tanza Road, Hampstead. When I opened it, standing by my bed with its fringed, turquoise cover, I found it was written on a scrappy piece of lined paper torn from an exercise book.

He sent sympathy on the death of Mr Kollerstrom. He said he hadn't written because he had been both very busy and quite sick with exhaustion, insomnia, colds and flu. He would be home in Ireland for the wedding of his young stepsister in the summer. His family had wanted him there so much they had clubbed together to pay his fare. He would use the occasion to seek help for his continuing ill health.

The letter ended with "It's interesting that….. and the page was torn out.

Nine days later a sentence was added:

"Will be arriving in Ireland on June 21st. I'm sure we'll meet during the summer.

Much love, Kieran"

This letter threw my emotions into chaos. It was one thing to have a correspondence relit with Kieran, working as a priest in South Africa, and it was heart-warming and joyful to see that we still had a relationship that included affectionate sign-offs. But it was still another thing, and far beyond any realms of possibility that we might actually meet again. I had fantasies that he might come to the flat for tea – after all, other visiting clerical friends had done so. I went into a frenzy of house-cleaning and restocking of pot plants and better china and glassware – presuming that he would notice or care about such ridiculous things. The underlying wish was to impress with the fact that I was now whole, analysed and had made it on my own. I could not even begin to admit to myself that our passionate relationship of love might reignite – nor that the fire, truly had never been extinguished. And yet ……and yet……

Nothing more was heard. I presumed Kieran had gone to Ireland to see his family and to officiate at his stepsister's wedding. Spring departed and summer arrived once more although not with the flaming heat of the year before. We were back to the usual weak sun interspersed with misery that typically defines the so-called English summer. In June the Queen's Silver Jubilee was held. We went to the British Council building near Trafalgar Square to see the golden coach drive past and drove around East London to see the tiny houses draped in flags, bunting and portraits of the Queen.

And then, in late July another letter arrived.

Dublin, July 18, '77.

"Biondina mia,

Yes, I'm back here and missing you terribly. Seven years, two serious accidents and many fevers later I'm admitting openly that I'm very much in love with you – openly that is to my medical doctor, psychiatrist and now to you.

I really believed in '70 that I was making the right decision by returning to Africa and remaining in the active priesthood. Now I'm not at all sure – My God how often have I looked at children and thought – "Pam and I could have a six-year-old boy or girl by now".

My dearest, I don't know if it's fair to be writing like this but you are and always will be at the centre of my life and my being. I'm sorry, very sorry for the searing pain I've caused you. I honestly didn't mean it – I thought I was doing the right thing. But life is more complicated than that. It may be that God has other plans.

And what of the now? Would you be willing to meet again and see where we stand? My psych thinks that it

will be necessary that we talk over things together.
Would it be possible for you to come to Dublin and if so
when? Perhaps you could let me know by letter or phone?

I love you dearly and always will.

Kieran"

If the previous letter had thrown me into disarray, this one caused complete mental and emotional chaos. I lived on vitamin pills and valium for two days then booked a 'red-eye' flight on the next Friday night to Dublin arriving just after midnight.

I had to tell Richard. He was uncharacteristically calm, understanding and affectionate and said he would give all the space and freedom that was needed. I should have been warned.

11
ORCHARD PINK WITH BLOSSOM, LOVE

The plane arrived in Dublin. If this story had been a romantic film we would have rushed into each other's arms. A string orchestra would have swelled in the background as we kissed and the lights faded.

The reality was different. I glimpsed Kieran through a wall of glass. He was wearing a blue jumper. The doors opened and we approached each other, not sure what to do. We had an awkward sort of embrace.

His first unfortunate remark, nervously blurted out was: "You've aged a lot!"

Was it any wonder, having had no sleep and no food for the last two days? The surprise was that I did not turn around and get the next plane back. We were both so tightly strung that we hardly knew what we were saying or feeling. In a kind of daze we weathered that storm and he drove me to the B & B that had been booked. I had firmly stipulated that we should not stay in any kind of religious institution, – saying:

"I am not going to skulk around any more monasteries!"

Not many love stories are pure Romeo and Juliet all the way. All too often the high points can descend into bathos. The following morning he came to collect me in an ancient long blue car. He was so nervous that he locked the key inside the car and we spent the first half hour of our precious reunion fishing for the door handle with a wire coat-hanger. At least it gave us something to laugh about.

Kieran wanted to show me places where he had grown up, including Ringagonagh College where he had spent happy times as a child learning Gaelic and listening to folk tales by the fire. We drove in sunshine around a green land, the colours iridescent in the sun. I was surprised at his reaction when an impatient motorist hooted at us. Kieran just laughed and said, "I love you too!" Used as I was to Richard's bad-tempered fulminations against other motorists it was pure delight. We went to Ring, and even met one of his old Masters. We had picnics of bread and cheese and tomatoes in the sun sitting on a borrowed blanket in the fields. There are photographs of each of us, kneeling on the rug, looking young and intensely happy.

We talked endlessly, sharing what we had done and experienced over the past seven years. We were seven years older and, while the depth of our love was unchanged, we needed to get to know the people we had now become. Initially we were affectionate but tentative. We hardly dared touch each other. It was almost as though each feared the other might vaporise into unreality and disappear. There was so much under the surface. We had held our emotions in check for so long that it was as if the love was afraid to climb back up out of the depths to which it had been banished.

I learned that far from forgetting our relationship, Kieran had thought about it constantly. He had prayed endlessly and desperately, promising to serve his God for the rest of his life in any possible way if we could only be together. He would go to Mazimhlophe, where with the willing local community he had built a church on a hill, and standing there at night, would shout my name out into the night sky. If only I had known. His name had been on a list to be the next Bishop of Zululand and he had asked for it to be taken off, saying that he was in love and would not be a reliable candidate. He had worked himself to a standstill, constantly

151

travelling throughout South Africa to attend meetings and give retreats. He spoke of the two serious car accidents which had put him in hospital for long periods. The first had broken bones and caused concussion, the second, a collision with a tractor loaded with sugar cane, had caught one ankle under the brake pedal, smashing the bones and severing nerves. He could have lost the foot. In an effort to prevent himself being crushed, he had bent the steering wheel into a U shape. He suffered a pulmonary embolism. The recovery took long months in a South African hospital, months of mud baths and physiotherapy in Belgium and further months in San Francisco learning to walk again. He attributed both accidents to emotional stress and tiredness.

After his return to South Africa, having done a year's further study in spirituality and psychology he set to work once more. With all his advanced training and his natural charisma, his reputation around South Africa as a lecturer and Retreat Master was growing. He was constantly travelling long distances to run courses for many different groups. On his exhausted return to the mission he would be greeted by his confrères with:

"So are you back here to do some work now?"

He would then find himself in remote rural areas, as he said, preaching to "three old women and a goat." And while the immortal souls of three old women and a goat were as important as the souls of any other beings, somehow he could not square it with his years of intense study and formation. He could see no clear future path.

One night, exhausted, stressed, dissatisfied and overworked, he drank too much in an effort to get to sleep. He found himself out on the wooden verandah of the mission house in the middle of a violent thunderstorm, shouting out into the night at the top of his voice-

"I'm leaving and I'm going back to Pamela!" He probably got some strange looks at breakfast the next morning.

As I had vetoed any more "skulking around monasteries', we stayed in a small hotel near Waterford on Saturday night. Hannah at Reception seemed to be smiling and sympathetic. By this time we had eyes only for each other and were glowing with love.

The next morning I awoke early. I put on my green dressing gown and went to Kieran's room next door. Opening the door gently I went in. He was still asleep. I stood quietly, just looking at him, as he lay there, peaceful, innocent, vulnerable and so much loved. Time seemed to have stopped. I could have stayed there forever, not asking for more than the joy of gazing at his dear sleeping form. He awoke. A smile broke out on his face. It was like the sun coming out.

No longer the passionate and turbulent young people of seven years ago, wracked with anxiety and guilt, we were now meeting as new beings. Our reunion had transmuted into something more profound, more tender and delicate than we could ever have imagined, fuelled and forged by seven years of suffering on both sides. At last we were free to be together. At last we had hope.

We went to church on the Sunday morning. We were both in a state of joy, amazement and shock. We spent a long time on our knees and discovered that, unknowingly in our turmoil, we had both been thinking of the words of John Henry Newman's poem, "Lead Kindly Light"

"Lead, Kindly Light, amidst th'encircling gloom,
Lead Thou me on!
The night is dark, and I am far from home,
Lead Thou me on!
Keep Thou my feet; I do not ask to see the distant scene;
one step enough for me."

As we set off for another sunlit day of driving, talking and picnics, the god of bathos reappeared. The long blue car began to make ominous noises. It had had many owners and had seen far better days. Our progress around south-eastern Ireland began to be interrupted by frequent stops at garages where willing mechanics tinkered with the generator and the carburettor. We were sent from one village to the next with promises that "Sure, Paddy will know how to fix it!" And in addition, as we drove, we seemed to be haunted by mysterious signs. Everywhere we drove the countryside was emblazoned with large signs saying "Jamborora". To me this looked like an aboriginal word. Kieran puzzled over it and said it certainly wasn't Gaelic. What was it and why were we being directed to it? Finally, turning a corner we solved the puzzle. On a large field were hundreds of small colourful tents, containing possibly all the Boy Scouts in Ireland. In our broken down, rattling car we had been following signs to a Gaelic Scout Jamboree. We burst out laughing.

By the time I caught the latest possible plane back on Sunday night there was no doubt in our minds. We were destined to be together for the rest of our lives and nothing could keep us apart. We were on a cloud of happiness. Our faces could not stop smiling. It only remained for Kieran to convince his Monastic Order, his brethren in Africa and the entire hierarchy of the Catholic Church of the rightness of his decision. I would have to tell Richard that we were breaking up the relationship that had sputtered on for the past four years.

Flying back to London on the plane all that was in my mind was the joy of knowing that our love was alive, the picture of a tall smiling Kieran at the airport with shining eyes, the memories of sun-filled picnics and happiness. The challenges and difficulties to come hardly seemed to matter.

And for Kieran too, who wrote the next day – "I do so miss you and love you until it hurts, yet I have that beautiful memory of the smiling goodbye at the airport."

Reality hit with a bump. The next letter from Kieran, while filled with so much love and joy, was also filled with details of all the other letters he was writing. He would have to be "laicised" – to leave the clergy and rejoin the laity, which would involve telling innumerable people about his decision, requesting letters explaining his application on medical grounds from various doctors and psychologists, explaining the situation to his brethren in Zululand, and to the innumerable Zulu friends, catechists and trainees with whom he had developed warm relationships during the past sixteen years. He was planning to beard the entire Servite Order at a meeting in Barcelona, if necessary, or Chicago, and had already begun collecting letters of reference and ideas about his future career. Eventually his request would have to be sent to Rome and on to the Vatican for an 'honourable discharge' and being Kieran, the soul of integrity, nothing less would do. There was no possibility that he could just walk out. The requirement was, after all of this, that he should have leave of absence for a year to be sure that the decision was what he wanted. We would have to wait for that year but in our minds there was no doubt and never had been. Had he been free we would have married only weeks after we had met.

I on the other hand had to come to terms with reversing the adjustment I had achieved over years of analysis and psychotherapy, where the emphasis had seemed to be on rooting out the love for Kieran from my heart, or at least living with the pain. I also had to meet Richard and tell him that our relationship was at an end.

From Richard's initial civilised and intellectual acceptance of the situation we moved on to rages, and blackmail. We progressed to a night when my front doorbell rang at midnight and every present I had ever given him for the past four years was piled up on the doorstep. I finally persuaded him to accept back at least the soft beds I had given Pud his cat and Ginta his dog, in fairness to them, but the gifts had to be sent back in a taxi. Histrionically, we would "Never meet again". Later there were sessions of wild telephone pleading to go on one last trip with him in his Fiat 500 down to Florence on a hellish voyage of dramatic farewell. This was soon followed one morning when I awoke to find a rambunctious white bull terrier puppy tied to my doorknob. Presumably this was meant to ensure the ongoing presence of Richard in my life. It was difficult for him and he was in emotional pain, but what was I supposed to do with such a gift? (In the end the problem was solved. My redoubtable landlady flatly refused to allow a dog on the premises. Pickles was returned to Richard and lived a happy life, going to work with him and spending office hours together with Ginta, tied to the legs of his office desk.)

Through all of this, daily letters arrived from my beloved – who never wrote letters, he said, filled with outpourings of love that I could not have dreamed of over the past seven years.

"Can I ever tell you how much you mean to me and how much I want to love and be loved by you. My beautiful bird of paradise, come what may, our love is all that counts."

We had exchanged little silver lovers-knot rings which upheld us both, and symbolised all that we hoped for. He wrote about the ring glinting in candlelight as he raised the chalice during his last Masses. He wrote about reunions with loved Zulu communities who were singing and dancing at his return, only to find the singing and dancing frozen and choked when he told them that he would be leaving Africa and not returning. He wrote about saying farewells to loved groups of catechists and nurses with a lump in his throat, feeling sadness but no regret.

156

"There was so much uninhibited joy when the kids and teachers saw me, dancing and singing and clapping, and then deadly silence when the news finally seeped through that my health was no longer suited to the climate. I just had to make my way back to the car crying with the people".

It was a time of intense love and longing, jubilation, overwhelming change and trepidation. Kieran wrote that he was "Afraid but not terrified", and that all his thoughts were of being together forever as quickly as possible. As were mine. I thought back to Mrs Bates and her Tarot Card predictions. She had predicted that in the summer – August, I would meet the perfect man. She saw him in Africa surrounded by African people. He would be completely certain of what he wanted when he arrived and would be driving a long blue car. He was. He would one day be involved in war zones, flying around in planes, and there would be a large gift of money coming my way before the marriage. It was all very detailed and specific and, completely accurate. I would keep a hopeful eye out for the large gift of money.

12

A THOUSAND GOLDEN APPLES, LOVE

Kieran arrived back from his trip to Africa, with bitter-sweet memories of all the farewells, with hope that his con-frères would continue to be as understanding as they appeared to be, and would support him in his plans, with undiminished love and hope for the future, with parcels and suitcases of beloved books and tapes, and with very few clothes suitable for a northern climate. A good friend in Johannesburg, realising this, had taken his own corduroy jacket off his back as he said goodbye, and had given it to him for the journey. One of our first forays was to Marks and Spencer to buy some jumpers, a warm coat and a dressing-gown which he had never owned. In the monastery he had had his monk's robe and in Africa it was not cold enough to need one. Choosing an anorak, he touched my heart by asking tentatively if he could have "One with a hood".

On my birthday, rather than tying a bull terrier puppy to the door, he bravely ventured into a tropical fish shop, and arrived with three presents, a pair of red sword-tail fish for the fish tank, a bag of water fleas to feed them and a golden lava lamp. He had also planned a surprise birthday meal at a small Hampstead restaurant with two friends, birthday cake and champagne. It was a remarkable effort for someone who had been brought up in a household without birthday celebrations or Christmas gifts. It would prove to be the first of many mutual birthday surprises during our lives. One of the friends present, later wrote:

"I remember meeting Kieran that day. He was sitting back on floor cushions telling stories about Africa. I thought you were the luckiest girl in the world. You both seemed covered in stardust."

We had blissful days and weeks in the Tanza road flat, bathed in love, sharing our favourite music, cooking meals, talking endlessly and tremulously, incredulously planning our future. Kieran was surprised and amused by my series of electric timers which 'exploded' every morning, switching on the electric heater, the lighted fish tank and the bubbling and hissing Teasmade machine. Everything gave us fun and shared laughter. There were a few alarms and excursions. A Zulu nun arrived post haste from Africa to persuade him of the error of his ways. We spotted her getting out of a taxi and stayed very very quiet while she rang the doorbell. Another couple arriving by taxi alarmed us, but proved to be representatives from the "Advent Group" a warm association of ex priests who came with friendship and advice. Other friends came round, to be introduced, contacts were made and suggestions were in the air – some of them even realistic.

Teaching was suggested – we went to Cambridge to see an encouraging clerical academic. Despite Kieran's excellent Masters Degree any University position would require at least another three years of study to gain a Ph.D. Work with overseas charitable agencies such as CAFOD (Catholic Agency for Overseas Development) was suggested – the pay was derisory and there were no current vacancies. The most helpful suggestion came from a friendly 'man about town' called Barrington to whom we were fortuitously introduced on Kieran's very first night back in England. He directed Kieran to a headhunting firm. From there in turn he was introduced to an organisation called "Chusid", an upmarket employment agency which specialised in helping highly qualified people who for some reason found themselves switching career in mid-life.

Chusid had premises in Fitzroy Square, and Kieran went along, full of courage and hope, confident in his abilities, but not at all sure what he might be asked. He enrolled, investing a sizeable percentage of the money he had been given by the Order to support him for a year. He was asked to spend the first morning taking a battery of psychological tests. One of the exercises involved writing an essay describing himself at work in ten years' time. He wrote that he saw himself in a big office, behind a large desk at the UN, overseeing International Aid projects. It is hard to imagine a more accurate prediction of the future that would be before him.

For the present, however, there was hard work to be put in learning how to write the best possible CV (Curriculum Vitae) setting out his education and career in the most favourable light and presenting his life's work so far in a way that would appeal to potential employers. He had good guidance from his mentor, a kindly and involved counsellor called Hugh Campbell. The most productive suggestion was to place his considerable qualifications at the end of the CV, and to present his previous life in terms of stories of achievements that he was proud of. It took some time to analyse these achievements and translate them into qualities that would be recognisable in commercial terms. It was followed by a series of 'trial interviews' – interviews that were real, with potential employers, but which were undertaken as trial runs, to sharpen and hone his interview technique and his presentation of himself. There were disappointments. Going out washed and brushed he came back crestfallen several times, having found that the field was not one he would be happy in, that there were no suitable vacancies, or that he had not impressed. The worst was an encounter with the executive of a multinational company which shall be nameless, who said, at the end of the interview:

"There's no job for you here. I just called you in for interview to see what an ex-priest looked like." Kieran came away hurt, shaken and appalled. A company neither he nor anyone with humanity would want to work for.

Meantime his sense of propriety and integrity reared its head. He decided that it would not look good, and might endanger his cause if he were to spend his waiting time living with me in the small Hampstead flat and set about finding a place of his own. He found a tiny one room bedsit in Kilburn, that slightly dingy island of North-West London, beloved of Irishman on the way up – or down. It had a brown bed, a brown chair, a brown carpet, a gas ring, a TV and an electric heater. It also had an extremely grasping landlord who came to collect his rent at 9 am every Tuesday. When he heard that Kieran had a lump sum of money stowed away he made the immortal comment:

"Who's getting the interest on that Mr O'Cuneen?" We laughed out loud. Getting interest on money was the last thing either of us had on our minds.

It seemed like a gift one day when Kieran discovered that his coin operated electricity meter was not recording. He did his washing, hung it up to dry so that it dripped onto a pot plant, positioned everything near the heater which for once he turned up to full power and felt that he was on a winning streak – until the washing fell onto the pot-plant, covering the clothes with soil and the entire edifice fell into the heater Thus are the wicked chastised!

There were happy moments during these months of waiting. A Zulu Musical called "Ipi Tombi" arrived in the West End. Kieran had seen it in Johannesburg and was keen for us to experience the Zulu song and dance together. We booked seats and he managed to get places in the front row.

We were enjoying the spectacle and the songs such as "Pata pata" when suddenly a member of the cast spotted him. Many of the artists were from the area where he had worked. Immediately the song changed and the cast began to sing, "Unogwaja is here!" (Rabbit is here!). He had a joyous reunion backstage after the show, asking after old friends and relatives.

The enchanting Irish harpist and folk singer Mary O'Hara emerged from years in an enclosed convent in Ireland and gave a moving recital in the Royal Festival Hall. I organised to go with Kieran and a group of friends. It seemed like a glimpse into a joyous future for us too.

Two more months passed and Christmas was approaching. We would spend Christmas with my ex-landlady Rosemary McCall in Eastbourne, now a good friend. I had gone down in advance. On his way, Kieran bought a copy of The Times. He opened it on the bus, and in it saw an advertisement that made his ears prick up and his hair stand on end. The European Commission was advertising for a translator between Gaelic and English. The successful applicant would need at least two other European languages. It seemed like a match made in heaven. Illogically he put his hand over the page in case anyone else on the bus saw it and applied first, which was, to say the least, unlikely. When he arrived he was hugely excited and over Christmas began planning his application and tactics.

The application was sent off immediately. Nothing was heard. But then no-one was expected to be working over the New Year. We had a frosty and hilarious Christmas with Rosemary who worked professionally with the adult deaf and was pioneering "Link", the first residential social courses for people deafened in mid-life. She was also a very intuitive person with an immense sense of fun. We departed, feeling that the New Year would bring good things. How could it not?

There had been no word from Kieran's Zululand colleagues. He was constantly in touch with friends in the Rome Headquarters of the Servites who reported that the required papers had not been received. It was beginning to look as though the delay was deliberate. Despite the apparent warm support he had felt during his African visit, he heard via the clerical grapevine the comment-

"You don't let your best team player go without a fight". This was complimentary, but hardly helpful in the circumstances.

As weeks passed the wait was becoming agonising. There was no job, interviews had dried up, and it seemed as though the laicisation process was being deliberately held up as well. The tension and uncertainty were beginning to tell on both of us. We were in limbo. We began to go to Mr Kollerstrom's beautiful wife Bridget for some counselling sessions which were gentle and reassuring. Bridget herself was still suffering from the death of her beloved husband Oscar and we became warm friends.

We went to stay in Essex with our Belgian friend Elsa and her husband the vicar, as we often did for the weekend. She was a strong and direct woman. And as a vicar's wife she knew something about planning weddings. One evening she said: -

"If you two are planning to get married you really need to do something about it. You can either have a full tribal wedding, and we can do it here at the Rectory, or you can elope, and have a sandwich at the pub. Which do you want?"

She informed us that we needed to decide on a date or nothing would happen. At least one of us needed to stay in the Parish for three consecutive Sundays so that banns could be called. It seemed like sensible advice.

We began planning the wedding. It was now March 1978. Kieran's bombshell letter of return had come in May the previous year. We decided on a date at the end of May. Whatever happened, we needed to be together. Marriage, after all is a contract between two people. We would have a Registry Office wedding followed by a creative blessing in the tiny Church of Little Braxted where we could include whatever readings and music we wanted. Kieran's best friend in the Servite Order would fly over from Ireland to take part in the wedding service.

Another question was his name. The surname "Rabbitt" was a mistranslation from the Irish during the 16th century, when the English made efforts to wipe out "Irishness" and repressed wholesale both the Irish language and the culture. Place names were translated into some kind of English, not always accurately, the singing of Irish songs was forbidden and harps were burned. Family names were compulsorily translated or mistranslated into English. Coming from a patriotic family Kieran was well aware of this sad history and like many Irish people longed to go back to what the family name had been. With research he discovered that the name should have been O'Cuinin, meaning not a rabbit but a young hound – the Messengers of the Kings of Ireland. He was beginning a new life. He would in any case have to give up his South African Book of Life, get a new drivers licence, and a new passport. This seemed to be the time to change his identity to one that felt more true to who he was, and to reclaim the family history. And so after much discussion, he visited a solicitor's office in Hampstead High Street and had a name change prepared by Deed Poll for very little fuss and very little expense. He walked proudly out of the office as Kieran John O'Cuneen. And to be honest, much as I loved and adored him, I was not completely looking forward to being 'Mrs Rabbitt'.

To prepare himself for any interviews or tests for the translator's job he went to Dublin to brush up his Gaelic – after all, even someone with native speaker fluency might be a little rusty after nearly 40 years and as he discovered, the orthography had changed. He was accepted onto a three week Government course, but it quickly became obvious that his Gaelic was of such a high standard and he was so highly motivated that Eamonn, his teacher taught him individually in return for a warming and convivial pub lunch every day.

Time was passing. Finally the letter arrived from Brussels. To his bitter disappointment it stated that his application for the Translator's position could not be considered as, despite his qualifications there was an age cut-off point and he was one day too old. Nevertheless, he was still convinced that Europe was where his future might lie particularly since he was already very familiar with Brussels and Belgian culture.

His teacher Eamonn, sensing his disappointment and despondency asked what was wrong. This was Ireland with its tribal network of relationships and contacts. Eamonn called in contacts. There was a fellow teacher whose father was a Senator. The Senator lived opposite Kieran's stepmother in Roscommon, and arranged an introduction to the Minister of Foreign Affairs. All were enthusiastic about Kieran's qualifications and experience and promised to back any application he might make to be part of Ireland's quota of positions in the European Commission.

I happened to mention the situation to a colleague in the British Council Scholarships department, someone whom I knew had worked in Brussels.

"Oh," she said. "It will take them forever to answer letters. He should just go to Brussels and talk to people from whatever department he is interested in."

And so it was that Kieran returned to London, and with money borrowed for the ticket, he set off, in naive hope, to beard officials at the Berlaymont in Brussels and persuade them that they could not do without him. With the innocence of the ignorant he stationed himself at the foot of the stairs leading to the Irish Commissioner's office. In the European Commission the Commissioners are like gods. No mere mortal can get near their thrones. After almost an entire morning he was spotted sitting in his chair by a friendly fellow Irishman called Liam Hourican who asked what he was doing there and invited him to lunch. As always, in the Irish tribal system they found that they had distant connections. Hearing his history and qualifications he said:

"Come back to the office with me. I can set up some contacts. We might have something for you."

He was rapidly invited up the stairway to Commissioner's heaven to meet Maurice Foley, Deputy Director General for Development in Southern Africa. Maurice was a bluff, jovial, hard-drinking Irishman with a ready welcome. This was someone whose down to earth language Kieran could understand from home. They immediately summed each other up. Maurice, from a working-class family, and with a hard-won background from the Trade Unions had evolved as a canny politician with a vision of the need for development in Southern Africa. Widely travelled in Africa, and with friendly personal relations with emerging African leaders such as Kenneth Kaunda, Joshua Nkomo and Oliver Tambo he saw clearly the need for Europe to give meaningful aid to the region. It was a time when European leaders were very aware of the need to become involved in the balance of power in Africa.

After a cheerful meeting when all of Kieran's details were taken and his CV produced he left with hopeful words ringing in his ears:

"You will be hearing from us. We will have something for you."

This was not mere nepotism. Ireland had only recently joined the European Commission and was having trouble filling its quota of posts for highly qualified multilingual officials. There were plenty of volunteers with African experience but no European languages, and many highly qualified academics without the necessary languages or practical experience. Kieran, with academic qualifications, multiple languages and African experience was immediately seen as a possible candidate to fill one of the vacant posts.

Elated with this news, he went that evening to see his Belgian friends, with whom he had been close during seminary days. They lived next door to the seminary and he had spent many happy hours there, as part of the family. Madame Paheau was a brilliant physicist, a wealthy widow with five daughters, all of whom had been like little sisters to Kieran during his years studying in Louvain. They were all extremely proud of him and he saw them whenever he was in Europe. Madame had always treated him as the son she didn't have, wrote frequently, and took every opportunity to shower him with expensive gifts- watches, clothes, books and music. It was the first time he had been able to visit them since his decision and he was looking forward to their love and support. What happened was rather different.

Hearing of his decision and plans Madame Paheau, whom he had thought of as a mother figure, considered carefully and then made her pronouncement.

"Alors, tu n'est pas exactement un traitre, plutôt une espèce de Judas!" ("Well you are not exactly a traitor, more a kind of Judas!")

This was not what he had been expecting or hoping. Kieran was bravely stepping out into an unknown world. He was open and vulnerable. Hurtful setbacks like this were damaging. We needed to cling together more than ever in mutual love and support.

It was now only weeks until the wedding. We searched for an engagement ring in the beautiful shops of Burlington Arcade. Having looked exhaustively for something we liked and could afford, we settled on a modest emerald surrounded by small diamonds. The benign owner of the shop refused to sell it to us. Looking at us fondly he said,

"I want you to go all the way up and down the arcade and look at every other shop. If you decide that this is really the perfect ring come back to me and we can talk."

Kieran very much wanted to have a ring too. It was hugely important to him. He took off the cross and chain that he wore, given to him by his father, and made from his mother's wedding ring. He asked that the gold should be forged into his wedding ring. It was a powerful and moving symbol of the depth of his commitment to our union, a commitment that never wavered.

I was engaged in planning the wedding, finding the perfect dress and shoes, typing out invitations, and cooking every weekend with Elsa, using some of her elegant but simple French recipes. With Kieran the blessing ceremony was planned and typed out, choosing readings we both loved.

"Though I take the wings of the morning and fly to the uttermost parts of the sea, Still thou are with me and thy right hand upholds me," had to be included, the psalm that expressed the unlikely wonder of our meeting, and which had comforted me on my initial flight from Australia.

We included a reading from Khalil Gibran's 'The Prophet"

> "For even as love crowns you so shall he
> crucify you.
> Even as he is for your growth

so is he for your pruning.
Even as he ascends to your height and
caresses your tenderest branches that quiver
in the sun,
So shall he descend to your roots and
shake them in their clinging to the earth."

We had found this to be true.

With mere weeks to go there was still no word from The European Commission in Brussels. Finally the letter arrived. It was opened with trepidation fearing yet another bitter disappointment. But it announced that a new post had been created specially for Kieran. Called "Southern African Regional Training Advisor," he would be in charge of monitoring all Regional Training programmes in six countries of Southern Africa, travelling widely to link countries with common aims and would be responsible for solving any problems as they occurred. He would be required to go to Brussels to sign his contract and would be given a three month period of training before going out to Africa. Once more he bought the cheapest air ticket available and went to Belgium to finalise the deal before anyone changed their mind.

Staying once more with the Servites in Brussels, in a simple room, he was given a medical, numerous interviews in English, French and Italian (but not Zulu) and was finally presented with his contract. To his astonishment he found that he would be earning exactly ten times as much as my graduate salary in London. I was a mere underling, one in a department of over a hundred. He would be one of a kind doing a job that had never been done before. It seemed as though he would no longer be in need of financial subsidy.

Kieran returned, still feeling some anxiety about entering a whole new field of activity, but confident that he would be able to do it with the training period offered. I felt I could contribute something too – as a Technical Training Officer in the British Council I had some knowledge of development projects and the administration of training programmes.

To cap it all, in a nervous phone call to a good friend and advisor, Fr Venanzio, in the Curia in Rome, to explain the situation, and tell him about our marriage plans, Kieran received the reassurance he needed:

"Vai avanti Kierano, La Chiesa comprende." (Go ahead Kieran, the Church understands".) And while that might not have been strictly true of the more dogmatic higher echelons of the Vatican, it was enough to calm his nerves before the wedding day.

13

SEED SACRIFICE COMPLETING

The morning of the wedding arrived. It was warm, sunny and bright in the Essex parish of Little Braxted. 27th May was the English summer that year – just one day of it. I woke up with a sense of excitement and unreality. In the elegant old Queen Anne rectory everything was ready. The food was out of the freezer, the rice was steaming, my hair was washed and washed again, the flowing cream dress was on its hanger. Kieran had been banished to a nearby house for the previous night together with Cyril, his fellow Servite and best friend from Dublin who would perform the blessing ceremony together with Vicar John. Barrington the best man had the rings safely in his pocket.

The tiny medieval church was like a garden burgeoning with flowers. Flowers on the altar, the window ledges and on every pew end. My harp teacher Tina Bonifaccio from London was coming to the wedding with Skaila Kanga, one of her young pupils, newly back from Paris, who would play the hymns, to avoid any threat of a squeaking and groaning harmonium.

No-one from either of our families would be present. Kieran was wary of the reactions of his relatives, and my parents felt that it was too far to fly from Australia for just one day. They sent a generous present which would pay for our short honeymoon in Ireland and we would meet later so that they could properly get to know their new son-in-law. They would host a dinner in Australia for good friends at the same time as the wedding and we would speak on the phone. Just thirty guests would be with us, friends from work and old friends who had supported and helped us.

There had been the usual wedding alarms and excursions to contend with. Father John the Vicar had taken serious umbrage the night before because we had unwittingly used words from the Anglican Wedding Service in our blessing, without asking his permission. Should we have contacted the Archbishop of Canterbury perhaps? Hurt feelings were soothed over.

Very early on the wedding morning we went into nearby Chelmsford for the official civil registry Office wedding. We made our promises for the first time.

I donned the empire line dress. The 'veil' was a delicate cream mantilla that Kieran had brought back from Majadahonda, after attending the General Chapter in 1968. Ten years on, it was the only gift from him that had survived the holocaust of the sad seven years. I was so glad to have kept it. The bridal bouquet consisted of three simple cream roses tied with ribbon. Kieran wore a dark suit and a silver-grey tie.

We arrived together. We walked hand in hand as we would do for the rest of our lives, up the path to the tiny church, through ancient grey gravestones, almost obscured by oceans of joyously waving white cow-parsley.

I hardly remember the service. The whole ceremony passed in a haze of incredulous happiness. It was surprising when Kieran invoked the Father Son and Holy Spirit as he slipped on my ring. I put the very special and symbolic wedding band on his third finger with equal love though less ceremony. Then it was over. We were at last officially One. We walked back down the aisle to the sound of the round "Rejoice in the Lord always". We had eyes only for each other.

The day was so warm and beautiful that the guests took their carefully prepared food out into the vicarage garden to eat on picnic blankets. The photographer was carried away and insisted we should crawl through laburnum bushes and stand on bridges gazing at each other for pictures until we were starving and begging for sustenance.

Elsa had brought a rose-covered cake from Belgium since we both agreed that the usual English fruit cake covered with white plaster of Paris left much to be desired. The harpist played while the toasts were made. The Best Man read out the telegrams mispronouncing Kieran's step-brother Porraic's name as Porridge. I played the harp and sang the old Irish folk song-

"I know where I'm going, and I know who's going with me,

I know who I love, but the dear knows who I'll marry"

At last we knew.

Finally it was all done. The blessings and the well-wishing were complete. In Barrington the Best Man's silver Jaguar we went to the airport to catch our plane to Ireland for the honeymoon.

When we arrived at Heathrow airport, glowing in the aftermath of our wedding day, a figure all too familiar to Kieran walked towards us across the concourse. It was one of the priests from Zululand, just landed and back on leave. Kieran introduced me as his wife.

POSTSCRIPT

Two months later the laicisation papers came through from Rome. We were invited to the Servite church in Fulham Road, London, to be married for the third time, this time by the Catholic Church. We were asked to come after 6 pm when it would be dark for fear we would be a scandal. It really seemed to us that there might be far more scandalous things going on in London at the time. Kieran was glad of the conclusion but we were so passionately and devotedly together that it hardly mattered one way or another. Perhaps tying the knot three times ensured that our union would be extra lasting and secure. Only death could part us now.

After the wedding we spent a short honeymoon in Ireland which from my standpoint, consisted mostly of being proudly introduced to relatives. We had collected my new Celtic harp which, much to our amusement made its journey back to London locked in the lavatory of an Aer Lingus plane.

We then went to Belgium for an icy three months. Kieran slipped and slid on ice and frozen snow every day on his way to the European Commission Headquarters at the Berlaymont during his familiarisation period. Then on to Africa. He rapidly mastered his new role, and over the years achieved a glittering career in the European Diplomatic Service. He rose to Ambassador rank in Africa and the Caribbean. He served in Swaziland (now Eswatini), Zimbabwe, Angola, Suriname and Trinidad and Tobago. He was chosen to be the European Special Envoy to Somalia in 1993 after the incident of Black Hawk Down, during the ensuing famine, and as Special Envoy to Rwanda after the 1994 genocide. He was a charismatic speaker. He could engage his audience and inspire ripples of laughter in any of his seven languages. Wherever he went he was loved and respected. His story-telling, his Irish jokes and his charisma made him universally popular. He learned 'diplomacy', but never lost his sense of fun or the common touch, and he made friends at every level of society and in every culture. We worked together in the Diplomatic world as partners in love and harmony for twenty-three years.

Kieran's struggle to decide to move on from the Priesthood stemmed from his intense sincerity and integrity. He felt that his vows had been taken with his whole heart and he was not a person to renege on those promises. He once said, "If I could negate those vows, then I might be the kind of person who would break marriage vows as well." He came to see in time, that perhaps God had different plans for him, ("Your life will change and change again" as was said in Mary's prophecy,) that there can be different kinds of love, and that together our vocation might be even stronger than his alone. Perhaps we should have listened earlier and more carefully to Mary's second prophecy – "Unite yourself completely in this love …."

His second career (or second incarnation as he liked to call it) enabled him to continue serving the African people he loved on a far wider scale than he would have been able to as a missionary in Zululand, disbursing millions in Aid.

I learned to be the "Ambassadors Wife" and in time acquired all the skills that involved. I supported him with all my love in everything he did and developed my own talents by studying psychology, Comparative Religion, art and music and teaching meditation wherever we went.

After retirement, Kieran forged two further careers, making exquisite jointed and inlaid jewellery boxes (see the website "The Ambassadors' Boxes") and travelling the world as a Cruise lecturer, enthralling audiences on subjects such as African History and Culture, and the Transatlantic Slave Trade. In everything he did, he was a thoughtful enthusiast.

Kieran never ceased to be a priest – once ordained one is a priest forever, even if not practising. In a crisis such as an accident or aircraft crash, he could minister to the injured and dying. As it was, wherever he went people sensed his deep spirituality and his priestly ministry and were drawn to him for counselling and advice. He assisted people in situations of life and death. He related to people from the heart. Everyone he spoke to felt that they were the only important person in his world at that moment, as he set aside documents on his desk and focused entirely on the human being in front of him. His kindness was legendary. He was a person completely without malice. Not only did he see the best in people, but he was a peacemaker, able to find positive and fair solutions to conflict, and would always support and help anyone anxious to advance in their life or career. His deep life of prayer flowered in human interaction. He was loved wherever he went.

****

Kieran died in grace, peace and serenity on 15th April 2023 after almost 45 years together.

It was 55 years since we first met.

We lived our whole lives with our arms around each other.

Our love deepened and increased exponentially as time went on.

His last words to me were "We are One. We will be together forever".

I profoundly believe this to be true.

There is nothing else that I wish for.

At his funeral Psalm 139 was read.

"Though I take the Wings of the Morning...."

The full story of our life of adventures together is told in two further books:

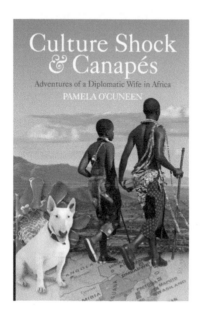

Culture Shock and Canapés
Adventures of a Diplomatic Wife in Africa
Pamela O'Cuneen, Quartet Books 2012, Chiselbury 2025.

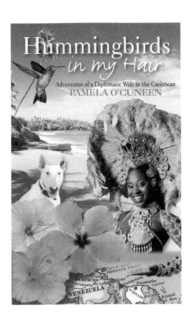

Hummingbirds in my Hair
Adventures of a Diplomatic Wife in the Caribbean
Pamela O'Cuneen, Quartet Books 2014, Chiselbury 2025.

BV - #0005 - 150125 - C10 - 197/132/11 - CC - 9781916556676 - Gloss Lamination